Credit Made Simple

Dollars and Common Sense

Written by Bliss McIntosh Green

Self Help/Finance/Money

The identities of some individuals in his book have been changed.

Published by

Passionate Pathways

8738 Arbor Creek Drive Ste B

Charlotte NC 28269

Send request and feedback to guidedbybliss@gmail.com

Name: Green, Bliss McIntosh, author

Title: Credit Made Simple: Dollars and Common Sense/ Bliss McIntosh Green

ISBN: 978-1-7351545-0-3 print

LCCN: 2020911493

This book is dedicated to my future and legacy in Christopher Green and Dunson Green

CREDIT MADE SIMPLE

INTRODUCTION

What is credit

What is credit? In several words and in a few, it is what you are known for or expected to do.

Credit is as credit does.

Credit gives and credit loves.

Credit grows and credit goes.

Credit can also dive and deal hard blows.

Credit soars and credit leaps.

Credit is meant for you to sow such that you abundantly reap.

What is credit? In several words and in a few, it is what you are known for or expected to do.

Credit dreams and credit thrives

Credit sets goals and credit changes lives

Credit empowers, but can cripple too

Credit is addictive, don't let credit ruin you.

Great credit plans, poor credit cries

You will always pay your debts when you are credit wise

What is credit? In several words and in a few, it is what you are known for or expected to do.

Credit is a whispered song to be shared and told

Mastered credit is a dying art of the disciplined and bold

Credit is a gateway to future prosperity

Credit is a resource and a tool for all humanity

Protect your credit in every single way

Credit is precious and is your financial power to say

anything that your credit would willingly afford

When used intentionally, in harmonious accord.

What is credit? In several words and in a few, it is what you are known for or expected to do.

So, what is your credit story? What credit say you?

Can we listen to your credit and know what you do?

Doth your accounting make mockery of the life you lead?

Doth your honor shine blameless with platinum exclusivity?

Are you even aware that your credit is telling on you?

Did you script a plan, and do you carefully review?

All that your credit is whispering for those who would only inquire

Doth it say you are the truth, or would it make you to be a liar?

What is credit? In several words and in a few, it is what you are known for or expected to do.

Let's keep it simple

Let's keep it real

Save money, and do what you say

You will start winning deals in a big way

You hold the future, you have all the keys

Make great choices and your creditors you will please

Common sense isn't common, because
Money evades the masses

Make sure your money has common-sense,
so you end up with stacks and stashes

Knowing is not enough, you must follow
this EXCELLENT advice

When you improve your credit, you will
change your entire life.

What is credit? In several words and in a
few, it is what you are known for or
expected to do. This is credit made simple.

-written by Bliss McIntosh Green

We live in a world full of options. You can opt to be included, or you can immediately be excluded. Our democracy is founded upon " Life, Liberty, and the Pursuit of Happiness". If you are reading this book, you are either out of the wealth inclusion huddle, or you desire to share this knowledge with someone who is left out of the wealth inclusion huddle. Many of us were not shown or taught how to create and maintain great finances with intention. Many have chosen to believe that their economic future is but chance. If you believe your financial future is a statistical probability of chance, what can you do? This is an AMAZING question. You can turn chance into change.

Making the financial changes we want is super simple. We have really bad habits of overthinking and over complicating things.

There is a reason we don't already have what we desire. We've made the "acquisition" of our dreams and goals, something complicated. I myself have been guilty of over complicating the simplest of things. I remembered the first time I learned about the law of attraction. The one thing about the law of attraction that I loved was the simplicity of it. The most common denominator between attraction and manifesting is our ability to actualize what we believe. Are your dreams possible for others, but not for you? Are there things that you desire, things that happen to other people, but not for you? Do you see others buying new cars, traveling the world, and buying homes? Do you see others opening brick and mortar businesses, investing on another level, and living their best dream life? Do you believe that you are worthy of what you deserve? Every day I must improve and control my mindset, and one day, you must control yours.

Are you procrastinating on making smart money decisions? Do you lack the discipline to budget because of your spending and lifestyle? Have you been trying your hardest and just can't make your credit score move further? Do you perceive that others are advancing in life, but not you? Do you feel trapped in your finances? Does your financial future seem way too complicated, unforgiving, and dismal?

Are your finances, or lack thereof, keeping you from your future lifestyle?

This over thinking and added complexity were often the hurdles that kept me from what I deserved in life. I had started my journey of personal development. I was reading all the fundamentals. I had been coached, and re-coached. I was crystal clear on who I am destined to be in life. I had created vision boards, and written

affirmations. I was reaching some plateaus, but I was not ascending. I was assured of a direct path to this "becoming or being", but I lacked the belief that I deserved to possess it. I protected this limitation mentality, which blocked all my efforts. These are what we call, limiting beliefs. They silently lurk in our subconscious mind and control everything we say, do, and feel.

The missing link of our being worthy of abundance is the number one thing keeping us from pursuing it.

In this book we are going to talk simple. We will talk about our desired financial future on our own terms, and our pathway to gain and retain our future lifestyle. You will see lots of references to our, us, and we in this love letter. I'm not talking about things I've studied. I'm talking about things I've experienced, practiced, taught, and received results from. Credit is simple, but it's not the easiest thing to obtain or maintain. Credit is made.

Credit can be made simple; if you plan for it and commit to it.

Sustaining radical financial change is a process that requires endless repetitive work. I've spent over 20 years as a mortgage lender. It is the reason I wrote this book. It was so easy for me to see how to create solutions for other's lives. It was much harder for my clients to bridge the gap from their present to their future. It has been taxing and complicated for many. I repeatedly saw that many clients would not rapidly proceed with credit approval once they were originally consulted. Most people are not willing to make the sacrifices, to follow the plan, do the work, be patient with the yields, and to wait on the results. We all know why. Working can be hard and complex. It does not feel fun. Sacrificing is even harder and is emotionally depleting. This was the defining difference between those that continued to rent, and those that met me at the attorney's office to sign their deed and pick up their keys to home ownership. Here is often the first crossroad between REAL change and just talking about it. Are you willing to do what others aren't to have what others don't? I must ask myself these questions repeatedly to gain progression.

I know what it's like to struggle. I know what it means to make impulsive split-second decisions that I could not afford. I know the despair of feeling emotionally, physically and financial trapped. I know what it's like to have drowned in the consequences of financial delinquency. I know what it feels like to sacrifice my way to financial responsibility. I know the pains and processes of creating a new discipline. I know the expense of educating myself and creating additional streams of income.

I also know the confidence and peace of sustained savings and investments. I know the freedom of financial options. I know what its like to see my stars in the sky, and what it feels like to take a permanent maker and draw that beautiful pattern. I know what it feels like to frame my star pattern and see what I've accomplished. I know the joy of this feeling. I know the enormous gratitude that is required to maintain this abundance. I know the greater joy of helping others go from no vision, to star gazing, to abundant star framing.

What dreams are you wishing on a star? Together, we can help you draw your dream, live it, and frame your dream on that star. We can all take our dollars and make them make sense, so that we can live uncommon lives. At the end of our lives, we should have a galaxy of memories that are framed in our minds and our legacy.

Abundance is meant for us all, yet, all of us are not willing to believe what we must achieve in order to receive our dreams. - Bliss Green

In other words, we make our own paths to future success complex because we want to skip the fundamentals. This is simple. We must not bypass the process in life, in living, and in our finances. Most importantly, we must make our lives as simple as possible so we can script a beautiful brilliant future for ourselves to live, on our own terms. The simpler our finances, the easier it is to manage and live our dreams. The simpler our lives are, the easier it is for others to follow us to the promised land. When we learn, we must teach so that we can live rich lives and never lack hand selected companionship.

If you are the only one you know that makes it to the top, you'll be there alone for a considerable while. However, if you take others with you, together you can change the topography for many.

In the book you will hear a lot of repetition. The simplicity of credit is just that; repetition. You are going to learn some tools, resources, and skills that will not only improve your money, credit, and financial future, but will change every aspect of your life. Simply put; you will receive repeated and abundant change in all areas of your life. You will be invited, equipped, and obligated to DO SOMETHING instead of just thinking about it all for the rest of your life…

When you are done with this book, you will no longer be watching the Jones' live their fabulous life. You'll be inviting the Jones's over so you can teach them how its meant to be done….

Most of the time, we attract and manifest who we presently are. This would be the fearful, insecure, limiting, unworthy, petty, reckless, unstable, emotional, whimsical, indecisive, imploding, angry, jealous pessimist that lives in our thoughts and in our core being. These emotions control our spending. YIKES! Maybe we are the kumbaya peaceful pipe toker, or the mindful prayerful priest, either way, maybe not in tune with our highest financial purpose and path.

On the surface, we appear to be, (maybe we even practice being), light and love, large and in charge, poised and profitable. Inside of us, lurking underneath it all is our human frailty and imperfection we desperately seek to mask. Our pride divides our soul from synchronizing with our expanding minds. One thing is certain, and two are for sure, whatever we focus on expands. What you are permanently perfecting in your finances?

So many people are on a financial emotionally charged roller coaster. People are living pay check to pay check and week to week.

Are you living just enough for the city?

The tourism and hospitality industry made billions with a "B" because of what they call "reckless spending." Consumers are reckless because they are emotionally charged. Depression, Holidays, Guilt, Birthdays, Fridays, and all the "Aye Aye Aye" party goers on any given day.

STOP IT! Stay home and read a book. READ and RE-READ THIS BOOK. Purchase it for all your friends and make them read it with you. In order not to spend, you must do something constructive with the time. Because spending occurs in everything involving electronics, you need to unplug your life. Declutter, read a book, or go for a walk. Write your dreams, Write your plans. The more you discover and learn, the more you'll figure out how to EARN. The healthier you are, the better you'll feel. Get involved in your life. That's what we all want to see on social media. We want to see you, living your fabulous life, instead of you complaining or commentating on the lives of others.

So here is my declaration of Credit Made Simple:

There are 3 actions steps you must take to make your credit and finances simple. You must speak your `truth`, you must reset your mind and budget with simple **affirmations**, and you must take repetitive progressive action.

There are 4 seeds of `truth` I want to plant as it relates to chances, credit, and changes. These are four seeds that I hope you will plant, even scatter to the winds, to grow as an evergreen forest in your life. In the workbook we will detail the discussion of how you pattern plant them in your life.

- Clarity
- Process
- Hope
- Influence

As you read you will begin to question your existing beliefs on money, credit, and savings. You will stretch and your mind will start to pivot. Progressively you'll begin to move forward in a positive direction. As you practice the verbs of simplicity, you will make mental shifts, and will increase your power. You will affirm your desires and intent for your future. All change starts in the mind. So yes, we will be programming our minds for excellent finances!

When you see the words COMMON SENSE – Please adhere to the aged wisdom in those words to live by. Write down how you have failed to apply the principle in your own life, and how you will apply it in the future. Write down how you feel about where you seen others failure to apply the practical intelligence of common sense. Write down ways to communicate with yourself and others about the consequences of ignoring common sense or reveling in ignorance.

When you see the words **Affirmation/s**— Please speak them out loud, confess it to another person, and write down those words that day in your own handwriting multiple times. Record them in your cell phone and play them back several times per day. **There is authority and power in repetition.**

When you see the term Simple Credit Verb, you must take immediate and massive action. Keep a record of your action steps and its impact in your day to day life.30-60-90 days. Write down your struggle to commitment, and your success along the way. Always make record of WHY your changes are necessary, and WHY you deserve their intended outcomes. Journaling is important.

Let us journey from our past, change the narrative in our present moments, so we can write the stories of our future. By now, you must be thinking this a personal development book; yes, why yes, it is! Without the process of development, we would all be savages.

It is imperative that you control the narrative.

CLARITY

“Your vision will become clear on when you can look into your own heart . Who looks outside, dreams, who looks inside awakens.”-Carl Jung

Credit is a system

What did people do before credit and money? They survived and thrived. They had trade and barter systems. They had honor and economic status systems. Finally, there has always been “street credit’. For all of you Game of Thrones fans, you’ll recognize this feudal street credit in the statement “A Lannister always pays his debts”. For the rest of us, our word must be our bond. There, my friend, is the simplicity of the credit system illustrated. Do you complete what you say you will do, when you say you’ll do it?

If you are living your life trying to avoid financing, then you are making things more complicated and more expensive than required. Credit is a system that is used to define what type of consumer risk you are to a lender. Using the credit system to your advantage can establish you financially, and help you create massive wealth. Not understanding and using the system poorly, can unravel good opportunities for financial freedom and stability.

It's not that you can't live and operate in a CASH society. The facts are that many people do. There are many online banks that are profiting from you doing just this. Our present-day financial systems are designed to collect fees, interest and to profit. When you operate in a cash only system, you are potentially limiting your purchasing power and missing out on opportunity. Present day finance modalities now prove that the credit systems, and investment systems are key components to modern wealth creation. If this book only does one thing for you, I hope the one thing is for you to understand that **if you change your credit, you can change your life.**

Nasar El-arabi the author of "Flip Houses Like Burgers" quit his job to be a full-time investor. I watched him transform his lifestyle. I watched how he has led other to do the same. If you follow him on social media, something he says often is "Know the Game". I love this saying because it is simple. Life can be simple, but we know it is seldom easy. In the game of life, we must stay focused on what we want, keep the main thing the main thing and understand how to make this thing work for us. #knowthegame

It sounds so simple to say this statement. Having great credit scores, strong credit content, and the behavior patterns that sustain them is tremendous WEALTH.

Credit is a simple system, but it creates complexities in people's lives. Understanding credit is paramount in building a strong financial future.

FICO

The Fair Isaac Company created by Bill Fair and Earl Isaac in 1956 was a computer software program designed to measure consumer credit risk. It later became known as the Fair Isaac Corporation. People refer to it as FICO. The company became publicly traded on the New York Stock Exchange in 1986. No lending process has been the same since. This new technology birthed an entire industry that would control the decisions of all future credit worthiness and generate billions of dollars in revenue for years to come.

Once lenders started buying into the program, other credit technology programs came to the market place. You may have heard of the Empirical or Beacon credit scores. There are many other names for the technologies. These credit analyst software programs are mathematical algorithms that quantify the risk of a consumer's credit worthiness.

Because so many different scoring technologies exist, there is often confusion about why credit scores differ from industry to industry. We will refer to this later in the book.

<u>Credit Bureau/Agencies</u>

For the technology to work, there must be a storage warehouse that holds consumer data. This is what the credit bureau does. It collects information about you every month from the lenders that extend credit to you. In today's present world we have three major credit reporting agencies. They are Equifax, Experian, and Transunion.

Every month your creditors report your payment history and loan data information to the agencies. The agencies then provide this content along with an assessment score to any inquiring lenders. The Credit reporting agencies only report the information they receive. They exist to report, and not to interpret decisions on credit extension.

As a consumer you should understand that credit reporting is locally influenced. Where you live in the country may determine the depth of information reported about you. Also depending on what you are applying for, there may be middle brokers that are re-selling the data from one of the 3 bureaus. It is important to understand that your credit sores may vary, and your information can and may be reported inaccurately at some point. Therefore, it is important to make sure that non accurate information is removed or deleted. You can do this by checking your free annual report at www.annualcreditreport.com.

Using any other consumer-based monitoring service may cost you money and may incur hard inquiries.

Credit Scores

In order to have credit scores, you must have credit. All creditor accounts are not created equal, and do not carry the same impact.

The type of credit you choose to apply for will have an impact on your credit scoring. Most consumers can apply for one of these types of accounts:

Revolving – these are open ended financing that you will continue to pay if the account is in good standing. (Ex- credit cards)

Installment Loan—these are financing with a pre-determined number of payments that will be repaid. (Ex. Personal Loans, Furniture, Education Loans)

Automotive- financing a car as collateral

Mortgage—Financing residential real estate as collateral

Many people get caught up in wanting to improve their credit scores. **The most important thing in your credit is the content of your credit.** The content of your payment history drives your scores. As you increase the longevity of your accounts with good payment history, your credit scores will improve. It is important to have a great credit mix. This is having different types of accounts reporting on your behalf.

The highest credit scores are for people who keep their balances low and are methodical with their finances. Consistency is key. There is that repetition word again. When you control your debts systematically, the easier it will be for you to apply for financing and get approved for the best terms.

Attention all Savings Shoppers:

These two words do not occupy the same space. If you are spending money, you are not saving it.

There is a time to spend, and there is a time to save. They just don't happen in the same account or at the same time.

When you are at the cash register and they offer you a discount for applying or their charge card'; decline the offer. Not all credit cards are created equal. There are major credit cards. These are cards you can use anywhere to purchase anything. These cards have the Visa or Mastercard logo on them. Then, there are retailer charge cards that you can only use at their specific store. Retailers offer these accounts to foster loyalty, monitor spending patterns, and influence marketing towards future purchases. Retailer charge cards often charge much higher Annual Percentage Rate (APR) financing terms than major credit card carriers offer. Having store credit cards is costing you more money in the long term. More reason to stick with the major credit cards and limit your spending.

Ask yourself— What simple thing can I do today to improve my savings and the content of my credit?

Credit Inquiries

An inquiry is when a creditor reviews your report for the purposes of extending credit. Anytime you apply for a loan, credit card, balance increase, utility, cell phone or financial service, your credit may be pulled. This will create an inquiry.

Be vigilant when applying for credit. Do your research first. Take referrals and recommendations. When possible, develop savings relationships first, then develop the loan relationship with a lender. Limit your inquiries. Use a free credit monitoring service through your credit card companies to keep track of your credit scores. Your goal is to be above average credit to excellent credit scores. This is likely about a 680+ score. If you know your scores are not this high, do not have your credit pulled for any reason, until you get there.

Only open new accounts that you require. Pay down or Keep you balances less than 30% of the credit limit. Make all your payments on time. Limit the number of new accounts you open at one time.

Credit Depth

One factor in credit scoring is how long your accounts have been open. We call this depth. Try not to close accounts that you have had for long periods of time. Keep the balances -0- but avoid closing the account because the longevity works in your favor.

Affirmation—I am focused on saving money, making all my payments on time, and paying down my debt. I have a great mix of credit accounts that create financial stability.

Credit is a tool

Credit is a tool, and we must master it to create a beautiful story for our lives versus a hazardous nightmare. Just like a power tool, you can use credit to create something spectacular, or you can use it to evoke harm and pain. Like any trade, you must use repetition to master the skillset of what you are creating. It is not enough to watch others use of their tool. Just like an infomercial fine print "results may vary" Credit is simple, but others make its acquisition and maintenance look easy. The use of the tool is key. For your individual credit system, and credit tools to work productively in your life, you must use them regularly. Credit is a tool, much like heavy machinery. While using credit, one should be sober and cautious. This requires you to be intentional. You must be intentional with whom you choose to engage in business.

You must know why you choose to invest in their business, and what the outcome or longevity of the business relationship will become. When you are careless in your use of credit and finance, this tool becomes a weapon of destruction and injury.

Like any power tool, its improper usage can create collateral damage that can negatively impact the lives of many.

Creditors and Lenders

Creditors and lenders are not your friends; nor are they your enemies. They all belong to an exclusive "help me protect my money and I'll protect yours" membership club. They use the reports to determine your ability to repay and how to assign interest rates per the risk they assess. For them, the use of the credit system is just good business. To you as a consumer, it is quite personal.

To continue with this "membership club" analogy, you are not a member of their club, but you can report any of its business practices to the governing authorities. The creditors/lenders choose when and how they report your payment information. They control if they report your history at all. The Fair Credit Reporting Act (FCRA) is there to protect you from fraud, or inaccuracies. It is important to have a basic understanding about the credit system, and how you impact it.

When the chips are up, and things are going our way, people see the banks as resources. When are chips are down, people see creditors as vultures and villains? Creditors/Lenders are telling your financial story, with the words you gave them. What do your financial commitments say about you?

Credit not Debt

Once upon a time, people saved for the items in life they desired. They did not acquire said items until they could pay for them. Long ago there was "layaway" It was the one thing that catapulted massive profits for retail shopping during the holidays.

Shop now, pay later, and get desired items after you paid off debts. It was a way to budget in a small increment. In our present economy, savings is far less sexy. It pales in comparison to the instant gratification of the almighty credit card! The consumer debt in our lives enslaves us into financial bondage. The negative belief systems we allow to control our choices and decisions can create poor financial habits. Our habits and practices do financially impact us, and those we love for extended amounts of time.

The goal is for us to establish functional and performing credit, but not debt.

We succeed in our Micro Economics.

When I was young, I often wondered how homeless people could survive on the streets? How could people who made little money afford to travel and own homes? The answer is that they don't have debt. What could you do without debt? Maybe a better question is, what would you *not* do if you didn't have debt?

It is not how much money you make, its how much money you keep. You can't save or invest significant sums of money if you owe significant sums of debt. My colleague, J. Parker, of the J Parker Network, teaches ordinary people how to begin investing in real estate. He teaches new real estate investors about prioritizing their life in microeconomics. How many hours per week do you have to work to provide yourself housing? How many hours per week to make your car payment? He always asks, "Do you have more month than you have money?" What are your alternatives?

How much money do you make per second? How much money do you make while you sleep? How much money would you need to earn to walk away from your job? How much money would it take for you to be financially free? He teaches people to stop trading time for money and start buying back their time.

I met Parker 6 years before I ever created the opportunity to own my first lot of land. I just never acted upon my knowledge. At the time, life was happening to me. I had depleted my savings in a recession. I was divorcing. I had small children. I had limited resources. Knowledge is only powerful if you act on it. However, the seeds were already planted. I went on to employ strategies that were profitable and diversify my investments today.

I'm saying to you that you must start somewhere. Don't be discouraged because you don't see immediate progress today. Don't allow the progress and success of others to distract you from your goals and intended path. Win in your daily disciplines of micro-economics and celebrate with the success of your macro-economics. Remember, savings saves lives!

Debt Traps and Convenience Traps

Any advance or loan that keeps you from paying it off and has a high APR (annual percentage rate) is a debt trap.

You are caught in a trap when you must continue something to survive. Payday advance loans are the worst.

Be not deceived, some financial institutions like banks and credit unions also offer payday advance lending.

You are being robbed and you have willfully invited the "*money absorption team*" into your wallet.

If someone told you, your own financial story in 3rd person using a "Once Upon a Time" reference. You would suck your teeth, smack them, and say "Wake up fool!"

We've all been fooled a time or two by the usurious expense of convenience. When we are willing close our eyes and walk (maybe run blindly) into debt traps or convenience traps, we are not a victim, we are a volunteer to the madness! Please, please, please **STOP!** The sacrifice you must make to **STOP** will be well worth the freedom of this debt trap.

Lifestyle Choices and ADDICTIONS

Do we really need to discuss this? ADDICTIONS are the ultimate poverty and debt trap. A friend of mine Tony Smith once told me, "Poor people have poor ways". I had never heard it put this way before. When I thought of this, I said to myself, this is so true. A perfect example is those who gamble and can't afford it. When you can afford your habit, it's called a "lifestyle" choice. When you can't afford it, it's an addiction.

Please note-- This goes for any and all the expensive and addictive lifestyle choices people make (Gambling, Alcohol, Drugs, Shopping)

There is nothing wrong with one off celebratory entertainment, or one ticket with 1 in 10mm odds on the Powerball over 400mm. I'm talking about out of control, every month, every week, every day behaviors.

If your bank account reflects your being issued "rainbow colored funny money", and you play scratch offs everyday.... STOP IT!

If you have no savings, and you play the numbers routinely.... STOP IT and slap yourself!

If you place a bet on the shade of gray the sun will shine tomorrow—STOP IT and get a head shrink!

If you are spending your gas money and lunch money on gambling, you need professional help, please call the hotline, and get a fiduciary to pay your bills and give you an allowance.

THIS IS INSANITY!! It is a well-known fact that most people who gain large sums of money go broke within a short time frame. So, if you are broke now, and statistics say you'll be broke in the future, pace yourself and SAVE! ☺ yes, I'm laughing, and it was a funny remark. In case you were wondering about my experience with gambling... I dated a habitual gambler for several years and my father still is a habitual gambler. Notwithstanding, on a serious note, if you are a substance abuser, or a bi-polar spender, please seek immediate *professional help and a new set of entertainment. Your life may depend on it.*

Non-Negotiables

People who have excellent credit pay their bills on time.

They are predictable and methodic with their spending and financing. They have a high utilization of credit. This means the balances on their credit cards are low in comparison to their limits.

Paying your bills as you have originally agreed to repay is non-negotiable. There are no excuses!!! Paying your bills every month, is the largest part of credit scoring and reporting, so it is imperative that you pay them on time. This is simple, and profound. Please pay your bills! If you can't afford a future payment that financing may create, please discipline yourself to walk away and refuse the purchase.

When you don't pay on time, you start incurring additional expenses in late fees, over the limit fees, and higher default rates. This commitment is fundamental to establishing and maintaining great credit.

In the poem at the introduction of this book, the phrase repeated says that your credit is what you are expected to do. When we say expected to do, we mean how you pay your bills. Do you keep your commitments? Do you pay some of the time? Can a creditor look at your history and feel certain you would repay based on your historical record?

Depending on how one was raised, one may have had a fluctuating relationship with money, priorities, and commitments. Money is an energy. It is to be respected and revered. If you are challenged in your finances, the first place you should look for authentic change is in your belief system. I read a book by Lynne Twist call the "The Soul of Money". In this book she speaks of the ways people save and spend, and how it is directly proportionate to their beliefs about money and credit. In this book she talks about systems based on scarcity, supply, and demand. She dares to suggest that we could live in a world of abundance and sufficiency. She talks of me AND you vs the propagated message of me OR you.

Our thoughts and actions are the only things that we can control. Regardless of what past ideologies we have about credit and money, we can create new thoughts and can change our future.

Affirmation—I control my thoughts, my spending, and my savings. I am responsible for my finances now and in the future. I am financially stable and thriving.

Simplicity Truth #1 is CLARITY

THE CREDIT SYSTEM IS SIMPLE- I can use this system to my advantage! Winning in finance is easy. Once I can clearly see and understand what the system is, who is it for, and how is it used, I will win with these systems. I must be clear and understand what is expected and required of me.

Simple Credit Verb—**CONFESS.**

Once I have discovered what is holding me back financially, I must confess it, own my present circumstance, and choose my desired future. In my present being and state of mind, I must be honest with where I am, and how I need assistance moving into my financial future.

Fault and Responsibility

Today, all the information of the universe is but clicks away on the internet. The only thing keeping us from our future lifestyle and financial stability is the willingness of our actions controlled by our minds. There are resources, records, coaches, classes, support groups, all available to help us further and progressively succeed and ascend. All we must do is act and keep taking progressive action. There is power and authority in repetition. One day, I saw a YouTube video clip of Will Smith talking about the words Blame and Responsibility. He mentioned how most people seek to blame others for why something did or didn't happen in their lives. Somehow this blame allows us to stay paralyzed and imprisoned in our personal despair. He then mentioned the word responsibility and how regardless of why something has occurred, we each are responsible for our own future. Our past is in the past, but our future is now. We must be responsible for creating the life we desire and move away from the circumstances of our past without blame.

https://www.youtube.com/watch?v=USsqkd-E9ag

PROCESS

Education and Resources

"When the student is ready, the teacher will appear". – Chinese Proverb

Have you ever wondered why schools don't focus on financial literacy? Considering how important it is to our financial survival, it's a wide-eyed wonder! Even more disappointing is that so many families and communities don't focus on financial empowerment. The average adult knows very little about budgeting and credit at age 18. Even fewer people know how to apply common sense to their financial decisions.

This is a narrative we must change in our families, in our communities, and in our nation.

Promoting Resources is so important. The real reason you are reading this book is that you are now destined to do more with your own finances by creating investments, affordable housing, employment opportunities, and legacy. You are also destined to share this information with those you know and those you will meet that need this sound guidance. You are also destined to #closewithbliss 😊 (sorry, I had to plug there)

Think back to a time where you had an "aha moment" that was the catalyst to a great future decision that paid off handsomely for you?

Who introduced you to that moment? Was it a family member? Was it a priest or pastor? Was it a book?

Now I want you to think about what you could have accomplished if you would have had that same epiphany sooner? How much further ahead could you be now in life?

You are given blessings in life, to share your light. Take your wisdom and share it to those who seek it. Make introductions to people with resources and to agencies. Connect people to what is next in their future. Planting seeds of sharing produces the strongest fruitful life!

It's not enough to learn a little. We all must constantly seek knowledge on how to earn, how to save, how to invest, how to finance, and how to increase our purchasing power. In this order." The more we know the more we grow. The more we learn the more we earn."

I've often thought that there should be more accessibility to financial literacy in plain sight. Upon trying to create such a platform, I discovered the meaning behind the aged wisdom of this Chinese Proverb. The universe is self-contained and abundant with opportunities and solutions. We must be willing to receive them and act upon them.

So many times, answers were right in front of us, but we could not recognize them. We were blinded by our ignorance, conformity, and possibly our pride. When one decides and commit to do something, all the solutions and resources will appear to accomplish a goal. "When the student is ready…"

Like many children raised in the south, I was raised underneath a church pew. Most of my origin references in life are biblical. The day to day wisdom in its contents and proverbs are awakening. Often, I refer to financial analogies from the bible because they would be hard for me depict otherwise.

There is a verse in the Bible that says, "God is a rewarder of those who diligently seek him". Hebrews 11:6

I personally find tremendous comfort in this scripture because as an adult, my understanding of "God" is highly evolved and expanded. To me, God is love. This includes all goodness, all abundance, all provision, and all prosperity. This also includes money, and money systems. This theory is simple to understand, but hard to practice. If I believe that prosperity, abundance, wealth, and freedom are for the asking and readily available, then why don't I readily command and possess it?

I like to think of prosperity, money, and provision as a fluid energy. I like to think of our education and wisdom experiences as vessels. The more wisdom and education we possess, the more prosperity and abundance we can process or retain.

Without the education and the experience of proven wisdom, acquiring prosperity and abundance is like holding water in our hands. It will only last momentarily. We will retain so little. I said all of this to say that we must perpetually learn so that we can retain what we earn. This is the reward of what we seek.

There are so many resources available to the public for creating wealth and establishing and maintaining great credit. All one must do is decide and commit to seeking the knowledge. When you are ready, here are some great suggestions for self-education.

This is your process. Use these resources, and improve your finances and life, over and over, again.

Write, Audio Record, and Visualize Your Affirmations and Intentions. —There is power in your intentions. Write them down. Record replay your **affirmations.** *Design your future. Keep a Journal.*

Post your vision boards on your bathroom mirror, your office desk, and your cell phone background photo. Hang it from your rear-view mirror in your car. Post it as your cover photo on your Facebook/Instagram pages. Wherever you spend the most time visually/physically, is where that vision board should be. Write your future, listen to your future, and see your future.

Read Books- Select personal development and self-help books. Read about savings and investment strategies. Read about elevating other areas of your life.

Ask, Employ, Engage- Find a mentor who has already financially accomplished what you specifically desire and ask them to share their path.

Hire a professional coach. Engage a group of peers that are striving for similar elevation and success

You Tube- Watch a video and learn "how to" improve

Public Library- Request historic references on wealth creation, debt, and credit

Cross Reference- There are so many resources available on the internet, cross reference all the opinions, get a majority proven system, and do what works best for you.

Repeat—Do all these things over and over, until it is all you think and do; until you are living the life you deserve. There is power and authority in repetition.

Affirmation-- I utilize all resources available for me to improve my finances and my life. I read to expand my mentality and professionalism. I am engaged in my financial future. I design the life I desire. I am successful because I am perfecting my process of improvement repeatedly.

Federal Trade Commission www.ftc.gov

This government agency is responsible for informing consumers on protection practices and enforcing the Fair Credit Reporting Act. (FCRA) The FCRA was enacted by law in

1970 to protect the consumer in fair and accurate credit reporting.

I would caution you to familiarize yourself with what the FCRA is designed to do. I would equally suggest that you note what it is NOT designed to do.

The credit repair industry is a byproduct of interpretations of FCRA laws. What may be common perception or common practice in the credit repair industry is not a true picture of what can and will happen with your original creditors.

Remember if you owe a documented debt, the creditor will eventually find a way to collect it. It is what creditors do. Unless you have filed bankruptcy, there is no limitation on how long a creditor can attempt to collect from you. The creditor is only limited in how long they can report negative information against you on your credit. Creditors by-pass this by selling your debts to other collection agencies and continue to report the collection as fresh new delinquency.

The predominant provision in the FCRA is disputing. When you dispute an account, your creditors must document where they are owed the debt within a specified response time, or the credit bureaus are required to remove the item from your credit report. Many times, the creditors are unable to comply within the allotted time, and the items are temporarily removed. When they get around to documenting the debts again, the items re-appear, causing further harm to credit scoring.

If you play the "smoke and mirrors" game of disputing accounts, they may vanish for a glimpse in time. When you settle on the debts you owe, and they will go away forever.

Affirmation I am using the resources available to me. I educate myself on how to make credit systems work to my advantage. I own my part in creating solutions, debt reduction, and credit availability. I am confident when negotiating with my creditors.

Budget for Savings

Savings and Credit reports are directly proportionate to one another. These 2 friends travel hand in hand.

The more savings you have, the less financial risk you will become over time. The reason for this is that savings and spending do not occupy the same space. They are a see-saw balance.

It is my opinion that if there were only one thing you could do to change bad credit, it would be to create savings.

When mortgage lenders look for reasons to lend you money, they are looking for what they call compensating factors. The amount of savings you have is one of the first things lenders are looking for. Savings is about planning and the habitual disciplines of the mind and habits of the wallet.

In order to create a savings, the first thing you must do is to decide to save and commit to all solutions that result in savings.

Admitting that spending and savings don't occupy the same space, is a hard truth to accept, because our economy thrives on household spending. If you don't protect your financial future, I can guarantee the government will not “bail” you out of financial demise or poverty.

For you to save you must do 4 things

- Sacrifice
- Budget
- Deposit
- Occupy Your Time

SACRIFICE. The important thing is to identify what you are WASTING your time and money on EVERY month and redirect those funds to your designated savings account. Operate on a zero-based budget. Take your bank statement and highlight all your entertainment and food purchases. Every time you get ready to go out to eat, or place an order online, ask yourself—is this worth not achieving your goal. The answer will be NO! Transfer that amount of money you were about to spend to your non accessible savings account. This way, you decrease your available liquidity to spend to -0-. Hence, a zero-based budget.

Work and Sacrifice are the admission price of the VIP section on the abundance train. VIP meaning (Valued Intellectual Property) You may still get on the train with general admission, but the VIP arrives in style and usually early. The difference between your arriving at your destined abundance and staying where you, are will be in your sacrifice and hard work towards becoming the VIP minded person that makes things happen for themselves.

Create and Commit to a **BUDGET**. This could be a simple short list or can be a full comprehensive excel spreadsheet. Write down a monthly, weekly, and or daily budget. Stick to your planned budget, and watch your cents, and common sense turn into dollars!

One of my favorite sales coaches, Tamara Bunte, taught me that you can't manage, what you don't measure. This is true for all aspects of life. Especially your money. You must keep track of where your money goes so that you can re-direct where you want it to flow.

DEPOSIT your savings in a bank you can't readily access without financing penalty. Online banking accounts, 401ks, IRA, CDs are a great way to save. Have money transferred from your payroll directly to these accounts. You'll never even miss the money. Don't ponder over the numbers on these statements, just let it silently accumulate.

<u>Occupy Your Time</u> in a Positive Manner without spending. While you are saving and getting financially healthy, now is a great time to get outdoors and get physically healthy! Start walking, jogging, anything that does not involve money. Now is a good time to take a part time job or start a side business. What one little thing are you good at that can turn into a profit? If working is not an alternative, let's raise our self-education consciousness. #level up READ A BOOK or several books. Get them from the local library and return them on time.

Remember you are not spending money when there is a low cost, or free alternative available. Mindless spending of money is a privilege for those who have already accomplished their financial goals. Once you have elevated your financial consciousness, I dare say you'll ever be able to mindlessly spend money again. Until we have what our hearts desire, we will have to keep our mind on our money, and our money on our mind.

You should find wealthy individuals to engage. Allow their lifestyle to extend and elevate yours. My friends have taught me that having great houses and toys is no fun without awesome people to invite over and share them with. Make sure you do so gratefully and authentically. The closer you become to people who are more well off, you'll find that most of them are always worried about SAVING pennies. The newly rich are seldomly counting the expenses....Wealthy people, count every penny.

Saving Grace

To further emphasize the concept, please note that the savings grace of every mortgage loan is in the amount of reserves. This is the money you have left after closing. We call this a compensating factor. Anytime an exception for a home loan is approved, it is the first compensating factor lenders look for. Savings Saves Lives!

Affirmations—I am saving my way to success. All my choices support saving for my financial future. I am willing to sacrifice for my desired life because I deserve it!

Fundamentals

The fundamentals of credit are to

- Get Established
- Pay as Agreed; or better
- Be Loyal and Consistent

- Create Longevity

When we bypass the fundamentals of credit, we sign up for heartache and troubles. If we follow this simple formula, we will create a rock-solid credit history that will give us so many options in life.

Getting Established is about taking responsibility or ownership of establishing your financial reputation. We each must own our story. Establish positive reporting relationships in your community with small business owners, utilitiy companies, local banks, and regional lenders is very important. The basic steps of opening a bank account, having utilities in your name, and other accounts go a long way for establishing reliable patters of future financing. These must be relationships that you own. The accounts need to be in your own name. We call these non-traditional credit references.

Pay as Agreed.

This is self-explanatory. PAY YOUR BILLS ON TIME PEOPLE!! It is the most basic expectation and requirement. There are not substitutions for your poor choices and bad credit history due to non-payment. This is how you know you are doing great, you can pay all your bills and save money too! Please, Please, please pay your bills on time!

Be Loyal

My sun sign is the Taurus. This zodiac is an earth grounded sign that is one of the most loyal on the planet! I understand why people feel that the Taurus is stubborn. We really aren't stubborn. We are some of the most creative and logical people on the planet. We are methodical and love a great plan. If we don't know the plan and can't anticipate the outcome of a circumstance or probability, we are not likely to follow in that suggestion or direction. The opposite is also true. If you can show us a great plan, and lead us to where we want to be, we will follow willingly and be most accommodating and flexible. When you work with professionals and institutions that are flexible to help you get established and teach you how to prosper, remain loyal.

Longevity

We all seek to find loyal relationships in life. Like the Taurus friend, your credit content wants you to be loyal and have longevity. When you open accounts, keep them open for the long-term reporting. Longevity is about sticking with the regularly scheduled program. Credit likes stability and predictability. There is power in positive repetition. Over time, your loyalty and longevity will pay off in creating excellent credit scores for you.

> COMMON SENSE - If you detour past the fundamentals in finance, your profits may be short lived.

Establishing and Re-establishing Credit

Establishing Credit today Is easier than ever before! You already have creditors that are not reporting to credit. (utilities, memberships, insurances, etc.) You just need to gain ones that do report to the bureaus. If you have –0- credit scores and not active healthy credit accounts, you need to apply for 3 types of credit.

- Local business references from the accounts you already have in your name that you pay monthly. This more like an expense and not considered debt.

This could be rental agreements, gym memberships, auto/renters insurance, utilities, etc.

- Secured Installment Loan- This is a loan made by a local credit union and or community bank. In fact, its not a loan at all. It is the money from your savings account transferring payments to an alternate savings account.

- Credit Card – If you can qualify for an unsecured card with out a savings deposits, this is best. Secured credit cards are the easiest to qualify for. This is where the creditor takes a risk on you but uses your savings as collateral.

The objective is to obtain new credit references, but not debt. Most lenders are weighing heavily on your repayment history If you do not have traditional credit references, you'll need to create them. This means that the non-traditional credit references.

One does not need to get authorized user accounts or add self-reported utilities. All you need to do is to establish healthy new accounts on your own. Remember this with opening new accounts. "all things in moderation."

There is often confusion about the fastest and most efficient way to create credit and to “repair credit”. As a matter of fact, I don’t like the term “credit repair” at all. I like to think of your financial commitments as fine works of art. Once you sully or destroy them, they must be replaced. Due to their nature as original works, repairing is not a sustainable option.

The best credit repair strategy is to focus on replacement

What exactly are you replacing you may ask? You are replacing your past choices with good new ones. You are creating new opportunities. You are creating new discipline patterns. You are maintaining those new relationships as you agree to. You are re-writing your financial credit and re-engaging your commitment terms is a more challenging task for several reasons. It requires the discipline of SAVINGS. It requires the ability to negotiate. It requires the commitment to follow up and follow through. I've often told this story to many applicants applying for a home loan. Credit reporting is much like growing up in a small town where everyone knows who you are, and a bad thing that happened to you early on in life. Let's say you move away from this environment, and come back for a funeral, class reunion, or other event. The only thing the town will be saying about you is the bad thing that happened to you as a child. You haven't given them any updated, relevant, or positive events to focus on. You would have to show them that you've gone on to become a great person that contributes to society and changes lives. Credit is the same way. You must not only fix the bad things that have happened, but you must create new fresh extensions of credit that are reflecting positively on your report. You must first replace the negative credit with positive credit, or your scores will struggle to increase, and you'll be delayed in moving on with your future financing options.

Results May Vary

"There is no elevator to success, you have to take the stairs" – Zig Ziglar

When I was in my early 20s, I read the book, "The Richest Man in Babylon" by George S. Clason. One thing I remember clearly was needing a systematic strategy to repay debt. There are not wrong answers, but there are better and faster answers.

- If you talk to 5 people about credit repair, you'll probably get 5 different answers on the fastest way to improve your credit. The one that you should take, is based on the specific person who can lead you to your exact destination where others have also arrived. If you don't follow strategic and specific plans of action precisely, your results will vary and possibly fail. Much like baking a cake, you must follow the recipe exactly to get the intended outcome.

To create a specific plan of action for your financial future

- Speak with a mortgage lender about qualifying for a home loan.
- Speak with a Credit Union about financing an automobile.

- Speak with a debt counselor before you incur additional debts.
- Speak with a real estate agent about investing in real estate.
- Speak with a financial planner about investing in insurance/ stock market

Negotiating Debt

- Negotiating Debt Is probably the #1 reason people pay a credit repair systems/person. Finding the right financial arrangement can be lengthy and weary. Most people do not want the burden of negotiating with past/recent creditors. There are huge opportunities for settling debts below their original terms and conditions. Please keep in mind that all a creditor wants is to be repaid their money. Create a solution for the creditor to get what they want, and for you to move on with your life.

- There is a difference in payment arrangements and an offer in compromise/ settling a debt.
- A payment arrangement is negotiation of a monthly payment schedule that intends to repay the balance of the debt in full. The payment arrangement is repaid over time. An offer in compromise is a negotiation of the debt balance to be cancelled to -0- balance for an amount less than owed. The offer in compromise is paid in a single lump sum.
- When seeking to repay a debt you must decide if you can afford to settle the debt in a lump sum; today or repay the sum over an extended time.
- In order to settle on a debt, you need to have this negotiated sum of money

already saved in checking or savings accounts. Payment is expected immediately.

You should not expect to request settlement of reduced debt with a payment plan arrangement.

When you repay over time, you will repay the full sum owed. When you pay a settlement, you create debt savings by paying in a lump sum.

When you are negotiating, make sure you get your agreement in writing. Document everything with a paper trail. The more serious the debt collection, the longer you need to document how and when you paid off the bad debts. This would be the case for anything that went through the courts. (Liens, judgements, and evictions)

Affirmation—When I am negotiating debt, I am prepared and have saved money. I always look for commonality that is in my favor.

Payment History, Late Payments, and Paying down Balances Early

It is estimated that your payment history accounts for almost 30% of your credit score reported. It represents the answer to an important question. Do you repay your debts as you agree to repay? This is a non-emotional response. Repayment is not a matter of sympathy or compassion. It is etched in stone. You either repay as you've agreed, or you do not. Creditors are not emotional, but humans are.

When you agree to finance something, you need to do so with as least emotion as possible. It will help you make a better financial decision. The simplicity is in the facts. Can you afford your new debt and save at the same time? If the answer if yes, then you could get the loan. If the answer is no, then you should NOT be financing. If you are unable to continue your savings budget, then what will you do when life happens? Therefore, you must make decisions based on facts not feelings, so that you can prepare to honor your commitments. Pay your debts on time each month.

When you make payments that are late, you really hurt your credit rating/score. The important thing to remember is that there are resources available to help you when you fall behind on payments for loans. It is important to act. Call your creditors and discover your repayment options. Consult with a non profit debt counselor. You can find some at the federal trade commissioner's website. The sooner you act and create a solution to move in a forward direction, the better outcome you'll experience.

Paying your debt off early is great! However, there are some things to note when you accelerate payments. On an installment loan, when you pay more on each monthly payment, you are paying the following month's interest portion. Be sure to send the principle reduction payment separate after you've made the required monthly payment. You can call the servicer directly and make principle reduction payments.

Affirmation—I pay all my debts on time each month. In fact, I repay my debts early.

Financing Important Things

OPM—when you borrow money, borrow it for things that are invaluable, or will appreciate.

Let's talk about mindset, honesty, and progression. The facts are that we each choose how we spend our money. We choose to finance things that we do or do not need based on our emotions. If we don't create debt or bad habits, there will be no need to fix debt problems. Have you read the book "The Richest Man in Babylon" by George S. Clason? Please re-read it. This means if you have already read it, do it again. If have not read it, buy it and read it twice.

GREED

We must learn to live within our means. We can have all things in a lifetime but not all things at the exact same time.

You know that you are greedy and or experiencing mental instability when you

- Make Purchases based on what other's receive or have (Jealous Jerry)
- Repeatedly overspend (undisciplined) (Big Money Mindy)
- Can't stick to a budget and or shopping list- (Whatever Wendy)
- Impulse Buyer (Midlife Crisis Matt)
- Feel the need to prove you have more or better than others (Holiday Holly)

- Deep Ditch Mood Swing Spender- (may be because you are compensating for a mental illness???)

Always ask yourself, is this worth the negative consequences this may create for me? Are my motives for buying these things from a place of internal peace and love? Are our decisions coming from insecurity and envy? Will I throw this away in the future? Is this something I really want, or are others influencing my decision?

If you can't purchase with planning, purpose, pride, and prudence, then you should not buy it.

COMMON SENSE- If you can't afford to pay for the maintenance of a thing, or the friends it will bring, don't buy it!

Interest and Annual Percentage Rates is the price you pay

No lender lends money for free. Lenders make money with the fees and interest they charge. The interest rate on any of your loans is the rate you agree to repay the interest on the balance of the mortgage.

The APR is the usually higher than the interest rate of the loan. It factors in all the cost associated with the loan over the life of the loan. This number represents how much the loan is costing you.

In case you were not aware, lenders do not extend you credit or allow you to borrow money out of the goodness of their hearts. They are making money on your debt with your expressed permission. They are making LOTS OF MONEY. The question is, how much money will you allow to be made on your outstanding debt?

How willing are you to negotiate and possibly wait to position yourself to save money in all finance's transactions?

Affirmation—I finance things that grow in value and are priceless. I only finance when it is required for a planned acquisition. I only take loans when I can afford to repay and continue to save money.

When to apply for financing

Patience is a virtue. So is knowing when to apply for credit. You know that you are in a good financial position to apply for credit because you will be able to do the following at the same time

- Remain Settled and Established
- Paying all your current bills on time
- Saving money

What does remaining settled and established mean?

If you have had multiple residences in the last 2 years, and at the same time, multiple jobs, you may be financially and or emotionally unstable.

If you don't have your own credit references in your name, lease, deed, utilities, and insurance, this needs to be your first goal.

How do you establish yourself? Save your money in a bank account. Apply for secured credit, then unsecured credit. Get utilities in your name. Get added to a rental lease. Maintain your employment with a consistent employer.

If you are not settled and established, you should not be applying for credit.

Applying for credit for "coin toss or grins and giggles" is a bad strategy because of the effect of the inquires on your credit. You should know that you will qualify, but just need to know for how much or rather the lowest APR you'll be offered. If you question if you'll qualify, its probably not a good time to inquire.

Get settled so you can start saving money. Chaining jobs and moving all the time is expensive...

There is nothing wrong with temporarily receiving assistance or having a co-signor. However, from a creditor's perspective, their preference is for you to financially stand on your own income, assets, and credit stability.

If you find yourself financially unstable, it's a good time to do some head/heart work and make sure you are emotionally healthy. If you need help, there are resources for you to get counseling and support. You are worth the effort of bettering yourself, so you can better your life. Life happens to us all, but we choose how we move forward with the cards we are dealt. We can write a new story for our future.

Please note this is a tough concept to convey to those who are experiencing "life" for different reasons. It is hard for a lender to tell someone that does not qualify for a loan in a non-emotional auto response. I add this token of wisdom because it is equally painful to be the messenger as it is receiving the message of denied approval.

How to rate shop

You only need one lender to tell you that you can qualify. Any additional lenders are expressing how they can save you time and money. The best way to shop for the lowest loan product, fees, and rates is to take the information that you have already researched and get a quote in writing that can beat what your bank was offering. If you prefer to work with a subsequent lender, then make a full application after you've gathered their facts. You will want to avoid having multiple lenders pull your credit scores.

The best time to borrow money is when you really don't need it.

Affirmation—I am confident in my choices when presented viable facts. I select the best professional that serves my desired results, and I take immediate action.

Procrastinating Fear

"There is no time like the present to gift yourself a brilliant future!" -Bliss M. Green

Procrastination is you wrapped in a big warm blanket on a cold windy day laying on your couch of mediocrity and conformity.

We find it comforting to do nothing. Procrastination is a paralysis that sedates fear.

For us to act, we must think. When we think, we must reason, or worse, decide. When we weigh options in reasoning, risk and fear always presents a very loud alarming tragedy that can stop us dead in our tracts.

Now this analogy is way over the top! We don't procrastinate when it really matters do, we? Or maybe we procrastinate so much in our daily non importance, we are unable to choose an alternate course of action when the stakes are high…

If at this moment, your conscience is squirming and crawling, you should read the book "You are a Badass" by Jen Sincero. The thing I love about her book is that it's self help for those who have not yet had their "epiphany moment", or can't yet see their stars in the sky, let alone connect the dots. When I read the book, I was struggling with my "epiphany plan of action" If I had to surmise her entire book in 2 *repetitive* concepts (*there is an undeniable theme here*)

1- Take any and all immediate actions TODAY – in your own way because you should
2- LOVE YOURSELF

Many people perfect the practice of procrastination. Particularly financially. There is power and authority in repetition. Earlier in my life, I had to consciously move away from sticking my head in the sand. Repeat after me, "**I AM NOT AN OSTRICH!**"

Just because there are no flashing lights, sirens wailing, or knocks on our doorsteps, does not mean we can remain complacent in procrastination by being in denial or indecisive. We must act toward progression.

When I was younger, I used to open my mail once a month. Checking mail was not my priority. I paid my bills at the same time each month, and that did not usually require me to read the details. Think of all the missed opportunities good and bad. I also now realize that because I struggled with concepts and assurances of abundance, financial security, and provision, that checking the mail was distressing to me.

One day I received a class action law suit notice in the mail that actually paid out. I now check my mail EVERYDAY 😊 I expect to see money, love, invitations, and gratitude, EVERYDAY. Today I have dealt with my certainty on abundance and provision, and I now EXPECT to see it in the mail.

COMMON SENSE– CHECK YOUR MAIL EVERYDAY. Not knowing and not responding never creates less of a consequence.

I have seen mortgage clients of mine delay on filing their income taxes out of fear of unpaid taxes and penalties/interest. Their delays only made matters worse. Had they acted, they could have saved time and money.

It is important to know that poor split-second decisions and not making decisions can impact our lives for a long time, especially when it comes to financing. Once a matter is brought to our attention, we must take immediate action.

Do you stay broke and busted?

Not having enough Funds, Over Draft Fees, Late Payment Fees, ATM fees, Transfer Fees all silently suck your precious earnings away. You should treat your money like children. You would not allow your kids to go with strangers, invite thieves into your home, or expose the family to known and unknown risk. We must be mindful of where all our money flows to at all times. We must protect our money one penny at a time. Keep the money innocent, happy, and productive. Teach your money how to expand and replicate itself. This would be done by savings and investing. If you have been guilty of allowing fees to eat at your finances, then you need to commit today to not incur any said fees in the next 90 days. This is everything from bank fees, credit card fees, late payment fees, over the limit fees, etc. Once you've made a repeat habit to save on fees, teach someone else to do the same. Limiting fees will level up your lifestyle.

Affirmation—My fear destroys my faith, but my faith destroys my fear. I am taking immediate and massive action towards my future financial goals today!

SIMPLICITY TRUTH #3- PROCESS. I must educate myself and follow the Process. I proceeded to allow my present circumstances, and I can proceed toward my future with patience and proven actions steps. I create viable solutions for improving my finances, make excellent financial choices. I take immediate massive action.

Simple Credit Verb—**PROCEED.**

I must keep moving forward with my plans. I must practice patience and stay focused on my financial goals and committed to the disciplines that will derive my desired outcomes. I must proceed and persist #simply proceed.

HOPE

"May your choices reflect your hopes and not your fears." – Nelson Mandela

If our repetitive habits and processes are how we program and reprogram our lives, then our belief is the remote control. Sometimes our beliefs and desires are not congruent. We are thinking the worst but "hoping" the best. In our past, we were probably filled with "stinking thinking". Our thoughts are drowned in fears and failure. Our minds often become cluttered with distraction and conformity. However, when we become mindful and present, we can gain appreciation for today and clarity on the future we intend to manifest.

As we work our process towards elevation in all areas of our lives, we must stay present and focus on the future. Particularly as you climb your way out of debt and financial despair. When we are making changes to our lives, all we have is the blind faith in HOPE. The crazy ideas that our souls whisper to us is enough to create sustainable life change. Without a new positive belief, how can we make permanent our new abundant financial plans? On days that you want to quit and spend your savings on tickets to Vegas, you remember your dreams and you stay the course in HOPE.

When you see others getting the things you want sooner, you run your own race in your own time, while you HOPE.

COMMON SENSE- When you compare your life to others you will despair. Make your plans and follow your plans in your own time.

The year before I published this book, my friend fell ill and ended up on life support. Normally, people's lives flash before them in an instance of trauma. For me, time was suspended. It was as if in that moment, time was a bridge between where I was, and where I wanted to be. It was time to act….

I've always been a writer. For years I said I was going to publish many bestselling books. I had just never acted on it. Just before my partner fell ill, we attended a small business expo in Charlotte NC. After the EXPO I had the opportunity to have lunch with the organizer, who is wealthy.

I'm seldom impressed with the money people have made. I am more attracted to how they've made their money, and what they do with their money. That day at lunch the self-made man told me something that stuck with me. It gave me hope beyond the fears of inactivity. I asked him, "When you meet people, what impresses you?" He replied, "If people would do half of what they say, I'd be impressed."

Two weeks later my life halted in the trauma of pending illness, and it was as if I instantly received divine clarity. As I prayed for the recovery of my friend, I prayed that I would deliver on all my wisdom and potential. I was afraid of the unknown future, and at the same time filled with peace and hope. While my friend was in the hospital, I began to write this book. My friend recovered, and life resumed business as usual for both of us.

However, I had to deliver on my intention. I had to publish the book.

I didn't tell many that I was writing a book. Those that I did tell were not overwhelmingly supportive. Some were even out right against the idea. The months passed, and my confidence in the book's purpose was being chipped away with my procrastination. I was being swallowed by myths, misunderstandings, and conformity. The dates kept getting pushed, but I still was making slow progress.

Then finally, I finished it! I also finished procrastinating the perfection of it. There is no greater feeling of accomplishment than to complete what you said you would complete, because you said you would. Particularly if it was something that you self-doubted. Acting toward your future fills your world with HOPE. The same is true for your wallet and your credit.

Do what you say, and tell everyone, "Hey, hey, hey—Look what I did!"

This is also a great time to note that nothing in life is perfect. Things just are. They are evolving. So, your hope is not in perfecting a project or a thing, its in seeing it through to completion and giving it your best, not to be compared to others. The same is for your credit and finances. They are not to be compared to other's finances. Our hope is to live the life we desire, not to live someone else's life.

When we embrace our new processes and HOPE through our financial journey, we must first show respect and appreciation for each of our original thoughts and understandings we inherited. We must uncover myths and we must implement new methods in our processes. Acting brings hope that propels us through to completion. However, first we must deal with our present beliefs that paralyze us and hold us back.

Misunderstandings, Myths and Methods on having excellent credit

Now that I know I must confess my truths, I must deal with those limiting beliefs I possess, and possibly the ones being told to me by others.

Our parents, teachers, and mentors have all done the best they know how to do. For us to progress and abundantly frame our stars the way we desire, we must learn from someone who has been to that same galaxy and framed that same star.

We must learn to uncover the myths/misunderstandings of others and

create new truths/understandings for our future.

Misunderstanding—Banks aren't a safe place to keep your money. Banks are safe if they are NCUA or FDIC insured, (up to 100k) and you hold them accountable for the money you deposit. All of this is done with a savings and loan, or credit union aka, the bank.

Myth- banks steal your money. They are profit centers, so they do charge fees, but your job is to find the bank that has limited to -0- fees for the privilege of hosting your money/savings.

Method- Banks are a great place to grow your money. You can get yields, dividends, and even interest on your money. *You must know the rules of engagement and play to win.*

Misunderstanding- The impact of credit inquiries and shopping around for lenders. Many people feel that they will keep applying with different lenders until they get the answer they desire. There is a small chance this could work, but most often, it has a negative impact on your credit score, and your ego.

Myth- You get a window of time to shop so your credit scores are not impacted. Credit scoring measures are not the exact for every person. This is mostly true for people with excellent credit. If your scores are below average, you may be negatively impacted.

Method- It is best to get 1 set of facts, then do your research. Once you re-adjust your expectations, then re-engage the application process. If you know you are quailed, tell the next lender that you are already qualified, but you are looking for a specific program, rate, or personality. Be brave and ask for what you specifically want. If you don't lead with this, you'll get more of the same responses, and or become more frustrated than when you started. Once you're confident, you've determined the product , the lender, and the specific loan officer you desire, have your credit pulled with them, then proceed with a loan.

Misunderstanding—All 3 credit bureaus should report about the same numbers.

This is a common misconception. The official bureaus warehouse the data content for your credit. They provide this information to the major industries that commonly request it- Mortgage, Auto, and Consumer. If you went to a mortgage lender, a car dealer and applied for a credit card all in the same day, you would be 3 different scores with the same bureau. If you are using an online credit monitoring system, (something like credit karma) those scores are based on consumer data and will likely be higher than a credit score that a mortgage lender, or an auto dealer would pull.

Myth- The same information reports to all 3 bureaus. You must check all (3) reports annually to make sure that the information reported is accurate and uniform.

Method—Start from where you are, and watch your scores increase to a significant level before you re-engage any lending process. For example. If your credit karma states a 607 score, then you'll want to wait until it says 680-700+ scores before you move forward.

Misunderstanding- lots of credit activity is good. Some people believe that constant activity of opening and closing accounts is healthy. It can harm your credit rating because it suggests consumer volatility.

Myth- Charging high limits and paying it off each month is helpful to your credit. You should keep your balances less than 30% of the credit limit at all times. This will give you the highest credit ratings possible. Its best to maintain low balances each month, and this include keeping low to constant activity.

Method—Steady Eddie has 800= scores. **People** who have the highest credit scores borrower money when they don't need it because they plan. They utilize home equity lines of credit and equity loans. They are very consistent and methodical in their spending. The periodically open new accounts, but seldom close any accounts.

Misunderstanding—You should have a ton of credit cards All credit is not considered equal. Individual Store credit cards have higher APRs than major purchase credit cards. Creating debt is not the goal, obtaining and retaining available credit is. Have you ever wondered why they attach so much savings to opening a new charge account? Its probably because of the interest they'll be charging you…

Myth- I should apply for several credit cards. You only need a few credit cards that have lots of available credit on them.

Method— Any new account openings should be for member benefits or better financing terms like a 0% APR on purchases and balance transfers. You should keep your original creditors open and active, but only add new cards that come at lower financing terms with higher limits. I understand some of your original cards may have annual fees, and you may consider closing those accounts because of this, but before you do, create the longevity with newer accounts first.

Misunderstanding- Qualifying with lower credit scores is a good thing. Anything you can afford that will accomplish your financing objectives is not a BAD thing, but all loans are not created equal. Please know that all lenders charge higher interest rates for people who have lower credit scores. This means that if you had slightly higher scores, you could save more money over time.

Myth—you'll pay the same amount in fees and interest with bad credit. The lower your credit rating, the higher the risk you are to a lender. This means they will charge you more for the loan product. They do this because there is a higher risk of delinquency and default for loans made to those with lower scores.

Method- Work on improving your credit first, then apply for financing. If you need to finance an item in a rapid speed, take the available terms, and know what is required to obtain more favorable terms for financing in the nearest future.

Misunderstanding—You can finance anything you want with good credit. The caveat is *all that you can afford to repay*! When you borrower money, you must document and demonstrate that you have the means to repay the debts. This is based on debt to income ratios. This is not based on performance, and or external budgeting factors. Its math, not method.

Myth- My income does not factor in my ability to qualify for financing. All lenders want to know you have the means to repay.

Even if they don't document the income, they want to see supporting evidence the income source is real. This usually involves documenting paystubs and bank statements.

Method—You can finance anything you can document that you can afford to repay with good credit. Budgeting and debt ratios are key! Live within your means and keep your debts to less than 25-30% of your monthly income. Make your documentation reflect your true financial capacity. If you are under reporting income and not recording/reporting assets, then a lender is not likely to mysteriously include them when qualifying.

Misunderstanding- #InstaCredit How rescoring or repulling credit works. There is such a thing in the mortgage industry as re-scoring. It is where a lender can force and update to the credit reports they pulled, and get new scores reflected based on new information. This creates a new inquiry.

Myth—Rescoring is a great plan. In theory, this could/will improve scores, but in application, it can turn into a nightmare because of the required precision in compliance on the part of the borrower.

Method- Patience is a virtue, and it is in your best interest to allow your credit to update naturally. I always advise my clients to wait 30 days after they last thing requested on their plan of action. This allows the credit to update naturally.

Misunderstanding—Avoiding the credit system after past failures or evading it all together. We often make the credit system complex, but it is quite forgiving. We must give it a better story to tell so that it will say the good things and not the bad things about our finances.

Myth- Establishing credit is hard to do, and re-establishing credit is harder**.** Starting over or getting started is simple. Create local relationships with credit union savings accounts.

Method- Open secured credit cards and secured installment loans. Focus on relationships and not debt. Use your savings as collateral. Establish payment histories on utilities and rent verification in your own name. Look for secured installment loan products.

Misunderstandings- You should accept all credit offers and finances as much as possible. Be selective on who you engage in borrowing money from. Only borrow money when it matters and holds your best purpose now and later.

Myth- It does not matter who I do business with. I can keep all my accounts with one institution. There is value in keeping your financial relationships as diversified as your investments. It keeps every party appreciative of your business and willing to give you their best. Loyalty exceeds competition when individual relationships exist. Always seek to develop banking and financing relationships with individuals at institutions. Relationships are important.

Method—Let your payment histories tell your story for you. Finance homes and land. These things retain value and appreciate. Do business locally, because more unique and traditional options are available. Do what you say and say what you do, and all the offers will come to you.

Misunderstanding- Home ownership is hard. Anything in life is as simple as you make it. Get a plan and work your plan of action.

Myth- I'll never be able to afford to own a home. If there is a will. You are the way.

Method- Work with a highly referred loan officer #PICK ME!

(Shameless plug #thisissimple #Ucan2 #closewithbliss #lendingbliss #mortgagegal)

Method- home ownership is a series of action steps. Get started on yours today with a local realtor and lender! Never be afraid to have a discussion on your plans. The sooner we speak with you about your goals and your resources, the sooner we can help you obtain your dreams!

Misunderstanding—I don't need credit to live my life.

You don't need it, but your life can be more complex by not having it. Are you still waiting in line at the bank to cash checks? Are you using automated cash cards/systems, hoping that major creditors and vendors will accept those forms of payment? What a hassle in this modern time.

Myth- If I avoid the system, I'll save more money. If you avoid the system, you'll likely spend more money. The system is designed to create savings lures to create/control spending habits.

Method—without credit, you are paying more for products and services. Understand the system and use it to your advantage. Know that using the systems is designed to reward you, and **vice versa.**

COMMON SENSE- You are worth the perfection process of your life; have patience and proceed.

Affirmation—I am learning the wisdom of money and finance. I cross reference options and opinions so that I deal in clarity and facts. I use these facts to develop new repetitive habits that propel me to financial success. I understand my deliverance is in my persistent practice of progression.

ACTION STEP- Read the book "Goals" by Brian Tracy. Write down the action steps to your financial goals as outlined by this book.

TRACK your intentional habits and decisions in accomplishing your steps daily and or weekly. Video, journal, and blog about the alternate decisions, sacrifices, and choices you are making to accomplish your new goal. Log how much you are saving at the end of each week.

COMMON SENSE- You are worth the perfection process of your life; have patience and proceed.

The Secret

Have you ever wondered why people are unable to sustain prolonged change? Why do human beings revert to Myths and Method mentalities? Why in our future do we succumb to our limiting beliefs?

It is because we are programmed to do so.

Unless we create permanent new habits, we will revert. It Is human nature. The only way to impact long lasting change is repetition. People have often said, "practice makes perfect" The reality is that practice makes permanent. What we think, we live. What we live, we teach. What we teach impacts and influences. Who we influence controls our future and legacy?

We must plan our future. We must be intentional in our choices. We must script our financial story. We must practice our financial ideologies with grave convictions, great ritual, and repetition. We must teach those around us about our financial priorities.

Those of you who have heard of, or possibly even practice the "Law of Attraction" have often wondered where the disconnect is between your present reality and your desired dreams.

The Secret is in our progressive repetitive action. Our thoughts are actionable. Our Time is Actionable. Our bank account is fluidly actionable. Our credit content and ratings are reflective and actionable.

The secret to our future financial success is our perfecting the repetitive practice of progressive financial responsibility. If I had to sum this up in 2 concepts it would be. Figure out how to Save more while you figure out how to Earn More. When we've mastered this, we continue to do it at a higher level. The Earning and Saving must never stop, we must never arrive. Once we do, we will revert. There is power and authority in repetition.

One thing I love about Lisa Nichol's book, "Abundance Now" is that she identified that common sense is not the most common thing. She states her motivation in writing this book was to break down her steps that led to her present-day success and abundance. She defines that success in life is a series of intentional repetitive process steps. She repeats to you what you've been avoiding listening to. The common sense that was screeching in your back ground all along like white noise.

"Experiencing abundance is not something unknown to us. It is something we are uncapable or unwilling to receive because we lack the wisdom or faith to accept it." -Bliss Green

Your Story, Your Life, Your legacy

Your Truth

You knew this chapter was coming because you are reading this book. You require an external authoritative expert to tell you what you already know in your heart and soul to be true.... YOU MUST BECOME AND ARE ALREADY SOLELY RESPONSIBLE FOR YOUR SPENDING, SAVINGS, AND FINANCING!

Working in mortgage lending over the last 20 years has taught me a lot about people and their ideologies on life and money. So many people have the wrong priorities to accomplish the things they "say" they want. Many don't even directly correlate their spending and savings as a part of their financial future. One must not think savings and wealth. One must live savings and wealth. It is a lifestyle choice.

I have this theory about life. You can have it all in life; but not at the same time on the same day.

I understand that this is easier said than done. We live in a day and time where keeping up with our friends and family on the next car, vacation, designer handbag/shoes is the highest thing on our priority list. One must remain at the top of the envy list. I do understand the gratification that acquiring "items" can bring. It makes no sense to allow yourself to be enslaved by envy and your ego.

When I was ready to stop with my shortcoming excuses, and get down to business, I had to be honest with myself and speak my truth. As will you. This is an ongoing process in life, which is why it must always remain in the present 1st person.

Say this with me:

- **My `truth` is that when I am ready to create wealth I will.** That last sentence ended with a PERIOD! There is no blame and there are no excuses.
- **My `truth` is that we are all manifesting our present and future circumstances one thought at a time, one day at a time.**
- **My `truth` is that my first step toward financial improvement starts with my thoughts around earning, spending, and saving money.**
- **My `truth` is that credit is just a story that I lived and someone else repeated about me.**
- **My `truth` is that most of the time, "they" repeat it accurately, but I may hate the way It looks and sounds.**

When we first accept that we control our thoughts, our emotions, our actions, our spending, our savings, and what we finance.... We can OWN the life we desire to live.

Now that we have been enlightened to a new way of thinking, will we live in our TRUTH or will we hide in denial and blame?

COMMON SENSE- don't practice lying to yourself. Own your truth; live your truth.

When we take one step….

Once we are perfectly clear on our present financial story, and what we desire it to become, we can understand the credit system and the part we play in the "game of economics". We have now educated ourselves on our options and are making calculated choices. We are on a progressive plan of action toward our future. We have a budget. We are saving money. We are spending intentionally. We are measuring our repetitive progression. What more is required for our liberation and transition into financial freedom?

Creativity

Be creative. We must create multiple streams of income. Each of us is talented, entertaining, or essential in many ways. Use your talents to generate additional income. What would an extra $300 per month do for your budget? There are 100 ways to bring in more if you put your mind to it. What would an additional $1000/month do for your budget? Finding a way to create income is the one step you must take to manifest unlimited solutions, resources, and wealth. When you take this step, the universe will move in your direction.

This income may expedite paying off debt. This may result in you increasing your credit scores. This could mean that you qualify for a better job, which could mean you would qualify for homeownership, or more! The possibilities are endless. Be creative!

All roads lead to Rome regarding this issue. Some paths to additional income do expedite your goals, much like an HOV lane on a highway. Choosing the right income producing activities can rapidly propel you towards success! The important thing to remember is that you must find joy in the creation and be at peace with the intention and effort required to earn. The activity must be harmoniously in line with your ethics and happiness. Remember WHY earning more is important to your future. Whatever you do, find a way to create and generate recurring money.

Affirmation to repeat— I am responsible for my thoughts, my actions, my savings, my spending and my life. All my choices and decisions are creating a wealthy financial future for me and those I love!

ACTION STEP-- Make a list of everything you are proficient in. You don't have to be a prodigy, but things you can complete accurately. Make a list of all things you enjoy doing. Make a list of things that people pay someone else to do. Look for synergy on those 3 lists and start a new creative side hustle or business.

A reason to care

Some people feel that credit is not necessary to have, OR to be concerned about.

Others are willing to "live their best life", but never can find the discipline to save for their major life investments. There will always be those that just don't have the economic resources to better their finances because in their present mentality and economy, they are trapped. Regardless of your economic stability, you are considered an associated risk that has an unpredictable future. Creditors rate you under certain assumptions and price or charge for their goods and services accordingly.

For example, people who utilize credit card offers, or apply for new credit cards can save additional money on products and services. We apply for new credit to save 10% in store. We apply for new credit to gain frequent flyer miles. A major credit card carrier brands itself as the card that pays you back. Our society is full of incentives for using our credit system responsibly. When you participate in the systems, you goal is extension of credit; not debt accumulation. When the credit system is used at its highest and best value, we can save time and money. When we avoid the credit system and or neglect it; the financial ramifications can be enormous. It matters, so we must participate with diligence

Affirmation-- My credit history matters to me. I will utilize credit as a tool to create solutions for my financial future.

The credit repair industry and financial accountability

The Fair Isaac Corporation, also known as FICO, was the first credit scoring module widely adopted in 1989. FICO has multiplied and replicated a million times since then to keep consumers guessing at the golden ticket to financial freedom. All the mystery of their algorithms has created a bi-product; The credit repair industry.

I like to think of the credit repair industry much like an American lullaby sang to a distressed infant. We love soothing ourselves into denial. We sing ourselves into hypnotic financial paralysis. We are kings and queens of evasion under the guise of delegation. WAKE UP AMERICA and take accountability for your actions! Start with a savings budget. If you dig yourself into a ditch of poor choices and debt, you can climb your way out into wisdom and savings. These two different mentalities can't occupy the same space. You can't dig and climb at the same time. You must choose and act. If there is a will, you are the way! The good news is that you don't have to waller in deep ditch despair! You can ask for help and climb your way back on top! You are all the solution that you require to fix any financial challenges you face.

I think sometimes we forget that our money, credit, and purchasing power, has a persona. We should treat our financial persona with intelligence and revered respect. I think some of us think of our financial persona as an invisible avatar that is cool and makes us feel good. However, when the bills come every 30 days, we conveniently dismiss its physical and emotional needs.

If we thought of our financial persona, as a controlling force in our lives, we could change our financial future.

We would never intentionally disregard or disrespect someone very important to us.

When we engage in reckless spending, poor choices, debt traps and convenience purchases, we often disrespect and disregard our financial persona. When we plan, budget, save money, invest money wisely, and practice accountability we respect and support the psyche of our financial persona. We often forget to love ourselves and respect ourselves in this regard. I get it, it's boring and so responsible. Trust me, your future self will thank the version of yourself that you are becoming by your even reading this book. **Love your financial persona!**

By the 90s, the credit repair industry had grown into a multibillion-dollar industry! It was so wildly profitable; the government created the Credit Repair Organization's Act in 1996.

This industry profits from your inability to take personal accountability, and possible indifference to knowledge. There is nothing about credit repair that one could not do for themselves. It is much like preparing taxes. You *could* do it, but most people would rather not think about it, let alone be responsible for its outcome. Now that you are aware of these facts, will you act? Will you control your credit story? Will you be like the masses and contribute to the profitability others gain from your poor choices or unfortunate circumstances? There is nothing wrong with paying someone to assist you, even out of convenience. However, if you don't have the disposable income, and an established savings pattern, you're better served learning the skill and doing it yourself, until you get to a stronger financial place.

Say this affirmation aloud with me—I am smart! I create great financial outcomes, and I have the discipline to create my dreams! I have a financial plan, and I follow the plan!

Marketing and Product Availability

As a mathematical statistic, you represent a future prediction of risk. Imagine the possibilities and outcomes of millions of consumers! Imagine the profitability opportunity! Imagine the future. Credit reporting agencies have realized and imagined. So much so, they create ways to package and bundle your risk opportunities to corporations as marketing resources. Credit companies sell your non private information to companies for top dollars. This is one way that we get specific goods and services, retail stores, and access to specific lifestyle provisions, within a certain mile radius of where we live and work. If you don't believe it, follow the franchise trends. When you see major brick and mortar retail stores coming to an area, you can guarantee that there are high income earners and disposable incomes nearby. If your favorite national coffee house just moved within walking distance, that was an algorithm at work.

Jobs and Cost of Living

As the economy grows, so does our cost of living! The same metrics that governs the incomes, credit risk, and preferences of consumers is the same data that dictates the expense of the goods and services that we consume and or are a beneficiary of.

In our society, we can't even get a good job without being able to maintain a certain credit score. Many people who are avoiding the credit system feel as if personal freedoms and opportunities are dwindling.

The insurance industry is now vested into monitoring all risk. Physical, Behavioral, and Psychological. They base our insurance rates on the future probability of your past known results.

Ask great questions, and plan!

If you are one that has not cared about your credit in the past, you are in denial and need to take immediate action. There are so many resources and tools available to assist you one step at a time. Your financial future will depend on it.

Affirmation to repeat--I care about my money and credit systems. I use money systems to my advantage. A penny saved is

a penny earned, and I love receiving money! I look for ways to increase my abundance daily

Living Your Best Life

A known way for you to be happy is knowing that you are accomplishing what you said you would do. I personally prefer the check list method. For me, making a list is the easiest form of goal setting. You should read the book "**Goals**" by Brian Tracy. It will help you get your priorities in written form and help you create the actions steps you need to take to accomplish each goal you set.

As it relates to your credit, making list and checking them twice is paramount! The best financial term for this list is the word budget. I like to think of budgeting as creating an outline for a nice painting and painting within the lines. You know exactly what you should be doing, and you clearly know when you are doing too much. Everything is clear and defined. Having a budget in writing allows you to accomplish your goals.

A wise person once noted, "When we fail to plan. we plan to fail." Budgeting helps us plan for success.

There needs to be a list for everything. We need list for our dreams. We need list for our legacy accomplishments. We need list for budgeting our time. We need list for what we desire in our lives. We need list for budgeting our net income. We need a list for budgeting our meals and entertainment. We need list for random happy thoughts.

The more organized we plan to be, the better the success of our plans. When we make these mental shifts of how we think about money, spending, and financing credit, we can literally write our future dreams down and watch them magically dance into our reality.

You can create the most basic budget on your own. If you need help, any HUD approved credit counseling agency can help you create a detailed budget that defines a new saving's goal for your future. The more detailed your budget, the clearer your results will become.

The more you write down your goals, the more often you'll notice that you are accomplishing them. There is enormous satisfaction in knowing that you said you would do something specific, then celebrating the day you do it. Frame your accomplished stars in the sky! Living your dreams starts with writing your desires down one idea at a time and acting towards each goal! This is simple. The book "Think and Grow Rich" by Napoleon Hill talks about the principles of achievement. Just by changing the way we think, we can change our lives. Once we put our plans in writing, and start to act upon them, we begin to take bold massive steps to create solutions.

When we allow our mind's eye to identify and visualize a new plan to execute, it goes to work for us. Therefore, the written plans, journals, and budgets are imperative to future success. We must also audio record our **affirmations**. Vision boards dominate our planning creativity. When we can see, hear, and give 3D dimension to our goals, the universe goes to work on its manifestation.

The universe does not require us to have our dots connected, but it does require us to take one step after another. All we must do, is allow. We must not interfere with our future intentions, by allowing our negative automated programming to override our mental adjustments. We must take our new resources and systems, and create an environment for them to thrive in.

This may mean that we must distance ourselves from people that don't serve our future interest. If your past friends are always spending money on meaningless things, you need a new set of friends, or you need to limit the time you spend with those people.

If you have people in your life that are dream snatchers; find a new tribe. We must linger to hope. We must cultivate the positive joy in our own lives and share that life with other people.

Affirmation to repeat—I set reasonable and clear goals. I make list and follow my budget. I am enjoying my life because I am accomplishing all that I set out to do.

Living a Legacy

We all know people that are "living the dream!" We all know people that are both young and old, who have nothing to show for their life but heartache and misery. The beauty in life is that we get to choose how we live. We get to live life on our own terms. We may not know when we will die, but we do choose if we die happy or miserable. We can choose to live a life of unfulfilled wishes or a life of purpose and legacy.

Legacy is such an important concept. A simple way to think of it will be how people will remember you. I like to emphasize the later part of that phrase. How will they remember you…?

Most people think of legacy as something you leave behind. This is the most traditional concept. If you don't live in the present, how can you create a progressive future past? Our legacy is something we create in the here and now. We define our legacy with our life's story. We define it with the impact on lives that we have touched and changed for the better. Those that we love, and those that loved us.

There have been many people in my life who have impacted me. There have been only a few people whose life has impacted my legacy. I have a mentor, that taught me most about shining like the sun, and impacting others from my own self-love. I had never met a person more generous and kinder. Almost everything they touched turned to gold. Almost everyone that they worked with or assisted prospered. They are an unsung hero. The most notable thing I could say about my mentor is that they don't seek credit, gratitude, or reciprocity. They live the life they chose, and they give from their heart daily, no strings attached. Their influence is enormous, yet its not something they orchestrated. It is a functionality of who they are, not what they do. I learned from them how to make my life simple and live it on my own terms. Their wisdom, influence, and presence in my life has helped me to create a world for myself that I don't even think I knew was possible. They are like my guardian angel, and for this I'm forever grateful.

The largest legacy and influence you'll ever have, is from who you've become, and who you help others to become.

COMMON SENSE—Every night forgive yourself, and purpose to do better tomorrow. Every morning show grace and forgive others.

Before you set the world on fire, you must first learn to identify and control your own flame. There is a concept that took me an enormous amount of heart healing to admit and adopt. Once I yielded to its path, I was able to allow the abundance of grace to flow into and through my life. This concept is:

We are all doing our very best, even me, on a bad day.

For me to embrace this, I had to acknowledge my own shortcomings, and remind myself that everyone else has them too. It meant I had to forgive myself and others. I have no problem forgiving people of unimaginable evil, but I've found it very hard to let go of their mindless tapping on my idiosyncrasies. Most people have majored in the minors of life. We give the highest priority to the most trivial of pursuits.

People are watching all that we do and say. No one is perfect. We do fit perfectly in one another's lives. The people in our sphere of influence rely upon us to become our best selves. We must create an environment for them to evolve with us.

We can reverse the "keeping up with the Jones' effect" and turn it into "the ripple effect". When we take a rock and throw it into a pond, it creates a ring of ripples. We can establish and maintain great credit. We can save for a down payment and buy a home and stop renting. We can save the money monthly to purchase a car out right vs. financing automobiles. We could take a part time job or create a side business. We can save for retirement and future education expenses. We can live our lives philanthropically. We can stand for social injustice, we can make a difference one penny at a time. We can create world peace.

It is hard to accomplish this type of enormous impact without financial resources. For you to leave your grandchildren and inheritance, there must be some savings left. For you to leave behind a substantial estate; you probably need to start with owning real estate. Every financial decision we make today impacts our legacy. The spirit in which we lived our lives, and yes, the things we leave behind, is the story people will tell of us when we are no longer here. Make sure that the good in your heart and head is not left unlived and un-gifted. Make sure that the things that are important to you, become important to those you love. Make sure that you have crossed off the major goals on your life list. Make sure that you share your hard work and goodness in life with those that are less fortunate and those that are "hypnotized" by conformity.

Our dreams are simple. The courage and ambition to achieve them are more complex. Be brave.

Make your life simple. Make your finances simple. Make your credit excellent and simple. This is how you live and lead your best life! Ensure the story others tell of you is the one you scripted. Today, pay your bills on time, and in the future, have something left to leave behind. Today is your legacy. Everything you dream of is within reach.

SIMPLICITY TRUTH #2- HOPE

Once I gain clarity about my finances, I can create a process to pivot from my past to my future. I can move forward. I gain the hope required to manifest my future. I am creating healthy qualifying credit today!

Affirmations— I forgive myself for making choices and decisions that did not serve me well in my past. I am free to make new choices and decisions that create the life I desire. I honor my commitments because I am a great person. I deserve the best, and I'm willing to work for it. I follow instruction from proven advisors. I believe in my future and that I am worthy of my future!

Simple Credit Verb—**PIVOT**

When I pivot financially, I turn away from past ideals and habits that did not serve me well. I define a financial budget that guides all my spending. I identify the financial myths and misunderstandings of others and my past. I follow new methods that get me positive future results. These mindset changes may be ever so slight, but they will make a huge impact on my life. It is with this hope, I can sustain every pivot required for me to turn around past choices and create any financial future I desire. #simplypivot

Affirmation- This day is the day I decided I was worth living my dreams, Today I am living my legacy. Today I access all the abundance credit and wealth creation can afford me. I am budgeted. I am grounded. I am full of hope. I am pivoting, and I'm excited about my future financial stability.

INFLUENCE

"You are the master of your destiny. You can influence, direct and control your own environment. You can make your life what you want it to be." -Napoleon Hill

Complete the Equation

Now that we understand that credit is a system. We understand that within this system, credit is a tool. We understand the tool can be used for good or can create evil. We still only know in part. Much like a premeditated game of chess. Most people engage credit like a whimsical game of checkers. The design of your credit structure should be approached with strategy. So, what is most important when dealing with credit? Your ability to repay your debts, out earn your expenses, and multiply your investments.

Credit is Queen, and her counterpart ruler is CASH the KING!

One half of the equation is income. The other is influence. As we improve our credit capacity, we must also focus on increasing our income and be intentional with our influence. We can influence our intentions and outcomes. We must control our inputs of influence. We must be intentional about our outcomes. We do influence how others treat us, and our ability to treat other people the way we desire. We can be benevolent and kind. We can afford ourselves a lifestyle that promotes health and serenity. We can lead others to give and become a catalyst for positive change. We can insulate our children and help them to reach their fullest potential at an early age. We can help others.

Once we have increased our income, we must develop our influence. It, like money, is an energy. It is not created nor destroyed. It must flow to us and through us. **We must define our own clarity, repeat our structured processes, experience the hope of our future, and influence others to do the same.** When we influence others to aid us in acquiring additional income streams, we empower ourselves. When we can influence others to extend us credit, it gives us purchasing power. When we can live the lives we designed and dreamed, we elevate and ascend. When we ascend to higher heights, we influence others to do the same.

Larry Wingate wrote a book "You're Broke Because You Want to Be". He suggests that its harder to fail at making money, than it is to succeed. What I loved most about his book was a theory called the Penny Energy. The Penny Energy talks about how you manifest your self-validations. It asks the question, " Do you value all money, or are you selective? How do you feel about finding a penny? Are you excited, or do you just walk by it? His theory is that your attitude towards any money is your attitude towards all money. Money flows to those who anticipate it and have excellent intention for it. If you believe that money will find you and greet you every day, then you shall find it. If you believe that money is easy and simple to create, then that is what you'll get in life. Look for the pennies. Create the value in your life.

Who is influencing you?

When I was a child, my father once told me about the power of association. I'm sure you've heard it phrased several ways. I heard it best when said, you'll be next. "If 3 of your friends are wealthy, you'll be next. If 3 of your friends are drug users/alcoholics; you'll be next."

The people we spend time with influence us. Even though we don't like to admit it. It is still true. Our family and friends have the highest influence. Their habits, ideologies, and limitations influence us.

If your family and friends are toxic emotionally and financially, you must find a way to limit your time from those behaviors. For me, family time has been a planned " Quality over Quantity" priority. The better I become, and the more financially accomplished I become, the better my quantity and quality time with family gets.

I'm not suggesting that you distance yourself or get rid of your family. I'm suggesting that you CREATE a life where you fill your time with positive activities and obligations, so your time with family will best serve you and be intentional.

Your friends are the family that you choose. There should never be a situation where you are choosing toxic people who don't serve your best interest at heart. No one is perfect, and people make mistakes. However, you know when you are in a relationship with people who are jealous and emotionally draining at their core, with no intention to change for the better. In case you are in denial, these are the ones who always take more from you than they give to you. If your "so titled" friends are never supportive of your accomplishments, talents, and goals. they are not friends. They are associates that are toxic.

We all have toxic associates. The unfortunate part is that it often takes some time to discover that is who they really are. Friends should support you where you are, but you must always be prepared to find new friends that can support you where you are going. In life, we are all travelers, and are not going to end up at the same destination at the same time. Sometimes we go with friends and family, sometimes we must go alone.

In a previous marriage, I was not able to develop professional relationships with men. This was very limiting for my mortgage business to say the least. There were other reasons that I decided to leave, but my business (and life) drastically improved once

I decided to leave my husband. I think I had forgotten who I was and what I once wanted in life. I forgot that I could still choose. The choice is always yours, choose your best life. Those that truly love you will support you, or they will make it easy for you to chose yourself. Either way, you win.

As it relates to money and finances, the people we spend time with influence us the most. When they go to the movies, we spend money and go with them. When they buy a new purse or shoes, so do we. When they go on vacations, we spend money and go with them. When they buy new cars, we spend and upgrade too. Even worse, some people spend money to keep the company of "toxic associates". People waste the MOST money being influenced by others or covering up their emotional insecurities.

You are already on a better and higher path, because you are reading this book. Be intentional with your time, and your money. Distance yourself from toxic people. If you are the toxic person (because people have distanced themselves from you) GET PROFESSIONAL HELP.

We can be a catalyst for change. Invite your friends and family to become financially responsible with you. Read books together. Get healthy together. Start saving. We can start investing in real estate together and influence entire neighborhoods and businesses. If no one in your circle will go with you, go anyway… their will be people waiting for you just around the corner.

COMMON SENSE – Care about all your money and other people's money too! Even Pennies!

A Penny for Your Thoughts

Where are you missing opportunities to receive increase? After reading about the Penny Energy there is not a day that goes by that I don't look for money on the ground. Most days, I find something. You'd be surprised how careless people are with coins.

What I noticed in my life is that my asking the universe to deliver me a penny a day was the first of my abundant request that I should be making, expecting, and having express purpose for. If I can have faith to receive a penny, how hard it is to bring in an extra $1000 per month? It's all the same energy. It is all love, intention, and influence. Find a penny, pick it up and all day, you'll have good luck!

Here are my top 4 places to randomly find money

Drive Thru windows

Gas Stations

Large Retail Stores

Near the Vacuums at the Car Washes

When we look at the structure of the credit system, we are really seeing a stage play foretelling our income and lifestyle we can afford. Without the ability to repay, there should not be an extension or advancement of credit. So, the

$1 mm question is, how can you increase

your income and your bottom line?

I want you to think of a growing green bush. Be the growing green bush. Your objective is to grow strong firm and fast. However, a part of this process is pruning. When you cut a bush, it grows stronger. Be the bush!

You need to learn this acronym and make it a song

#CUTit #CUTit #CUTIt #CUTit...... (you need to cut it)

CEASE—what can you stop, cut back, or cut out?

UnEARTH—What income streams can you build or create? Discover how to build a foundation of income

TAKE OFF—Level Up your collaborations, investments, and earnings

#bethebush #cutit

Cease (#CUTit)

Again, I say the 1st thing to access abundance is to find out where you can save money. What are you willing to sacrifice or make concessions on? Can you transfer balances to a 0% credit card? Can you eat at home more? Can you cut back the frequency of your spa treatments? Can you give up a round of golf? Can you stop all online purchases? Can you give up a meal per day? Can you eliminate annual fees and or transaction fees? Can you lower your cell phone coverage plan? Can you switch to online banking with -0- fees? Where can you create savings? What excess can you eliminate?

<u>UnEARTH</u> <u>(#CUTit)</u>

Where can you create cash flow? We all have a talent or likeable feature. How can you monetize this? Can you cut grass? Can you start a wash dry and fold service? Can you bake cakes? Can you play an instrument in your town square for donations? Can you tutor a child? Can you clean houses? Can you do light handyman services? Can you do auto mechanic work? Can you start a podcast and sell sponsorships? Can you start a YouTube channel and get subscribers for sponsorships?

Can you write/blog? Can you interpret a language? Can you meal prep? Can you apply professional make up? Can you sew? Can you clean gutters, repair decks/fences?

What can you do to bring in an extra $500-1000 per month?

Take Off (#CUTit)

Use your knowledge, gifts and talents to not only increase your earnings but to launch you into abundance. #levelup.

Who do you know that can increase your efforts? Who is missing in your life that will help you grow? Find them, befriend them, hire them. Allow these people to inspire and improve you.

When you are in growth mode, you employ new modalities and access new resources. Do you need to work on your concentration, breathing and meditation? Join a fitness studio or yogi community.

Do you need to discipline your time, personal space, and organizational skills? Hire a life coach who can improve your results. Work with the coach that can provide you a client reference that has the results you desire.

Are you filled with frustration, anger, sarcasm, and pessimism? Do you take little things and make a big deal out of everything? Are you always on edge and have high anxiety? Do you have a problem with everything and everybody? You *maybe* (ARE) the problem.

Do the math…. If this is your mental state, then you are probably making choices and decisions that don't best serve you. Your emotions are controlling your financial decisions, crippling your wallet, and jeopardizing your future finances.

Find your way to local counseling and work your way up to professional mental therapy. Its ok to admit you are "not ok". Its not ok, to know you are "not ok", and do nothing to help yourself be the best "not ok" person you can be. What the world needs now, is love sweet love, and less "not ok" people. This is a different book, on a different day. Read "I'm OK -You're OK" by Thomas A. Harris

I share this with you because I spent a considerable part of my childhood and young adult life, feeling not ok. Without the help of my #sanitysquad, I would have been a much different person. My life has all layers of complexity. Some I've inherited, some I’ve chosen, others adopted. Without my #sanitysquad I would be mentally trapped and would never be able to help myself or others. These are my confidants and mentors. With much prayer, love and support of the framily (family + friends) and my #sanityquad,(even at times a great shrink) I’ve been able to be the best, “not-ok” person I can be.

Now I know what you’re thinking. That is not a positive and progressive thought. You may be thinking this is trapping yourself into being “no-ok.” To this I would respond that for me to pivot from where I’ve been to a future happy place, I must first accept what I am, where I am. As I move towards being ok, I’m peeling back the layers of “not-ok” so that means that yes, I’ll be several versions of "not-ok" on my path of elevated love and light.

Some days I'm awesome sauce! Some days I'm "dripping sauce". Some days I get lost in the sauce.... 😊 That's ok! For me, my higher power has a name. Its JESUS. Jesus knows exactly where I'm at, and "the way my universe is set up", I have created an automated mental, emotional, and financial GPS. With very little effort, I can redirect myself back to my north star.

Regardless of your spirituality, you must have resources, people, and rituals that can reposition you when life takes the breath out of your lungs, and or knocks you down. If you lack these relationships and rituals in your life, you will likely become easily frustrated and burn out. This is your first step in recovery and moving you into the life you deserve. Get an emotional and mental support system. Be gracious to yourself. Experience grace.

Will some people ever be ok? Probably not, because they don't really want to be ok. Don't let that person be you. Keep moving towards improving every day. We can all strive to prioritize our mental and emotional health, and be the most prepared, resilient people we can be. This is imperative to pivoting and elevating to the new life we desire. The one where we become "OK". Life is a journey, not a destination…

Pay Attention and Win Together

While we are discussing credit, income, and influence, let's bring everyone we can bring along, this path in every way possible.

When you see others massively struggling in areas of their life, if you love them, (and have the financial means) you'll purchase this book and give it to them, with love. 😊 You'll hire a coach for them, with love. You'll take them to counseling, with love. (no matter how uncomfortable it makes you feel, or what it stirs up in you) You'll point them in the right direction, with love. This is influence. Influence with your love.

Don't allow those you care about to struggle while you ignore their pain. They are NOT OK, and one day, their life may depend on your love and influence...

This can be as simple as your inviting them to "your group" as a sign of support for you. Invite them to AA. Invite them to homebuyer education. Invite them to anger management. Invite them to whatever it is that can support them. Maybe they are just lonely. Invite them to your game night with friends.

One of the first ways to physically see that there are deeper or larger issues at play in others' lives is to notice when people hit big financial highs and lows.

Don't turn a blind eye. Your influence can save a life.

Ask your friends, and family, to support your endeavors. Create a lifestyle and community that will support these endeavors. Understand that your friends and family may not be on the same personal growth path as you are; and may not be supportive. Be prepared to grow and move forward with or without them. This is what it means to take off. Are you willing to take off?

COMMON SENSE – follow the golden and platinum rules financially, physically, and emotionally.

Have you committed to be the bush and grow by using the acronym #CUTit ? Are engaging ways to cease, unearth, and take off? Your $10mm or next level question is **how can you use credit to increase your earnings and wealth**?

Credit is a resource

If you change your credit you can change your life. It will not happen overnight, but with intentional "chess like" moves; you can make radical life changes. For all of you that are reading this book on behalf of "someone you know", please listen carefully. I'm whispering this portion of the book to your brain so that you'll pay careful attention.

People are watching what you do, not what you have, and not what you say. People are watching what you do. Your actions are your influence. When you have more, you should be doing more.

When you earn more money, you should be investing more money. Your money should create a return on investment. When you have excellent credit, you should be in the position to extend credit to others by way of creating affordable housing. You should own rental properties. You should have ownership in a business. (even if it's just shares of stock) When you are better than blessed, and your financial cup overflows, you should be pouring into the lives of those who have less or have nothing.

It's not enough in life to have; we must do. Money is an energy and it must flow.

Credit is a resource. Use it wisely. Invest your resources into things that extend grace, cultivate equity, give opportunity, and multiply blessings. Do more than just accumulate things for you and yours that will just collect dust. Own Houses. Build and Invest in a business that employs people. Create opportunities not only for yourself, but for others.

When we look at the top 10% of the wealthiest people in our nation, they usually share this one thing in common. They have mastered how to leverage systems, tools, and resources to create an EXTRAORDINARY life. I submit if they can; you can too. #Ucan2

Credit is not only a system, and a tool, it is a resource that can change your life, and your world. It is the resource that creates influence so that you can impact the lives of others.

COMMON SENSE – *build bridges not walls. Allow your credit to create not destroy.*

SIMPLICITY TRUTH #4-
INFLUENCE

When I change my credit, I change my life. I am influenced by those I spend time with. I am influencing others. My impact and legacy will be to teach others to live free, possess power, and win on their own terms!

Simple Credit Verb—**Lead.**

When my life begins to change, I gain an audience of people who are haters, cheerleaders, and witnesses to the abundance that is available in this life. I can influence and lead, or I can choose to hide in conformity and mediocrity, I will choose to lead #simplylead

Credit Made Simple

Credit is a bridge on the path towards financial freedom. So, for all of you who didn't know your next steps to financial freedom; may the force now be with you. For those who have excellent credit and are comfortable, go and create something that will expand your reach and be a blessing to another soul.

In the words of Biggie Smalls, "If you don't know…. now you know…!!!" Now you are REQUIRED to do something. You have been given a series of serious adulting to account for and accomplish. You must speak your common-sense truth, you must reset your mind and budget with simple **affirmations**, and you must take repetitive progressive action.

Reading this book could be another thing you will do to procrastinate, or it can change your life! You decide what you do with this information that you are now responsible for.

Ask yourself, of the following truths, which one created a "sunrise" experience for you? Which one of these was a blinding light, that you already knew, but have been painfully avoiding? Which one of these truths has been a twinkling star that you've been wishing upon, but is way high in the sky, just beyond your grasp?

Remember the 4 fundamental yet simple truths to adapt in your credit story

- Clarity
- Process
- Hope
- Influence

Now you are exposed. Your mind is forced to acknowledge the exact location of your current financial choices and decisions. This is your square one. This is your present existence. Is your credit strong? Does your credit influence? What is your credit influencing? Where is your mentally? Where are you emotionally? How is your bank account corresponding to your mind and emotions? Are you in denial? Are you living beyond your means? Are your ideals of finance uncertain and unreasonable? Are you fully aware but paralyzed by fear and conformity? Are you fuzzy on engaging resources and options? Are you presently unaware of the bridges and gaps that must be built to move you into your desired financial future?

What must change in our mind for us to step into our future financial life and lifestyle? Create a new script for your life. Reprogram the negative obsolete dis-functional data that is piloting your life. Write to your future self in present tense. Think aloud, but in ink, and paper. Write your I AMs. Your **affirmations** should ALWAYS be Present, Positive, and Progressive. Read the book, "What to Say When You Talk To Yourself," by Shad Helmstetter. It will help you with re-programming your mind. Use the **affirmations** in his book as a starting point, and then write your own. By the companion journal for this book and script the life you want. There is power and authority in repetition.

I took a public speaking and book writing class that gave me the crystal ball clarity for this book. The teacher suggested that we do a 90-day **affirmation** challenge. He suggested that we write down an entire page of **affirmations** everyday for 90 days straight. Any day we missed a day, we had to start over at day #1. It was one of the most simplistic yet full on lie detecting discovery exercises I've ever attempted. This process is a slow-motion plan that rewires your brain and reprograms your life. We must practice drill and rehearse our future mentality, actions, and inputs.

We will either create our own solutions or we will validate and complicate our problems.

This is the entire villain/victim syndrome. It took me 6 months to complete this first 90-

day challenge. I made tons of concessions, modifications, allowances, and excuses for why I couldn't sit down for 30 minutes each day and write my future.

I made these excuses to myself,

" I mean, come on!"

"Cut me some slack, I was busy doing my job!"

"I had responsibilities as a mom."

"I needed time to shut down and reboot."

"I was tired."

"I was constantly being interrupted."

" I couldn't get up any earlier. I couldn't stay awake at night later than I previously did."

"I'd do it twice tomorrow"

I said all these things.

Some days I cried through it. Some days I soared through it. I revised the words several times to speak to my soul; to command my mind. It took about 60 days before I got my core themes down pat. I learned how imperfect I was. How was I going to manifest these intentions into my life? I couldn't even commit to the darn notebook of **affirmations**, let alone the VERBS required to bring about permanent lasting change. I felt defeated, and "not ok". The beauty of the exercise is in the process of defining your gratitude, and your hope every day. It is the ultimate GPS for pivoting. The exercise caused me to be transparent, fragile, exposed, and introspective. I learned how to extend myself grace, to keep trying, and yes to start over. I discovered how to forgive my own shortcomings. I discovered that I would need to do the same for others. In case you haven't noticed there is power and authority in repetition. We can practice perfectly, or we can perfect whatever it is we practice. Therefore, creating **affirmations** is so important. Even in our finances, we must reset our minds and pivot to a new healthy script and dialogue of abundance and wealth principles. We must create rituals that sustain and ground us financially, emotionally, and mentally. At all times, we must give thanks for our journey; past, present, and future.

So, what is it going to be? Will you hit the snooze button every day of your credit and wallet life, or will you wake up, and take repetitive life transforming action?

What is credit? In several words and in a few, it is what you are known for or expected to do.

Write the script on your financial future. Set your own expectations. Get **clarity** as you line up your sky full of sparkling dreams. Use resources to create the **process** that will help you connect your dots. Pivot your mentality and the way you see your financial existence by changing your mindset to create **hope** for your future. Harness your ability to manifest **influence** over your life and others to change your world! Take this outline and frame your stars for all to see! Teach someone else to do the same. **This is credit made simple.**

Wherever our square one may be, we get the opportunity to start fresh each day. We can ascend to higher heights, we can elevate and evolve. We can redefine our income and credit story. We can create a legacy. We can influence. I hope that the simplicity of this message has inspired you to engage the credit systems, tools, and resources available. I trust that I'll be flooded with testimonials from determined people who will refer me to others and create massive success for themselves.

These things are not just high-minded ideals. These concepts and actions have changed my story and my life. I have watched how my coaching, counseling, and career expertise has guided and improved the credit and lives of others around me. Grant yourself access to the extraordinary abundance, equity, and prosperity that you deserve. Share this simple system with others. May we all live an abundant life that is simple.

COMMON SENSE–*Make your life simple and happy. "An ounce of prevention is worth a pound of cure!"*

May we all experience world peace, and own the piece of the world we choose, on our own terms.

Say this with me

"I am manifesting the abundance of love, light, prosperity, and peace in every dimension, especially my money. I am teaching others to do the same. This is simple. My credit made simple. "

<3Bliss

Thank you so much for reading this book. Be sure to purchase a copy for someone you love and purchase the workbook to design and manifest the future you deserve.

How to qualify for your dream house

Often the number one thing people need to improve their credit for is to purchase a home. I'd be remiss to write a book on credit and not spell this out. Every client is considered a risk to a lender. It is only a matter of what type of risk you represent. Your documentation tells the story about your ability to repay. It is imperative to make sure your documentation is ready and cast you in the highest and best light.

Well qualified clients have the following

- **A stable 2-year residence history with a lease or mortgage history of no late payments.**

- **Consistent 2-year employment history or documented wages on a w2 and or federal tax returns.**
- **IRS documented qualifying income**
- **No late payments within the last 12 months reporting on credit.**
- **No disputed accounts with balances**
- **Debt to income ratios less than 45%**
- **Money for deposits in a bank account for over 60 days and or retirement funds.**
- **Savings for at least 3-6 mortgage payments after the closing.**

Of course, the industry makes exceptions to these standards. The good news is that there are loan programs for those who are well qualified, and those who need a little grace. If you need help overcoming challenges, or planning for a home purchase, we'd love to help you! We have community partners and resources to help every client type.   Please contact us at www.lendingbliss.com

Made in the USA
Columbia, SC
05 February 2022